Personal Details

Name ______________________________

Address ______________________________

____

Email Address ______________________________

Phone # ______________________________

Notary Log Book Details

Log Book # ________

Log Start Date ________

Log Finish Date ________

NOTARY RECORD

Printed Name and Address of Signer:	**Phone Number:**	**Thumb Print:**
	Email:	
	Signer's Signature:	

Service Performed: ☐ Oath ☐ Acknowledgment ☐ Jurat ☐ Other:	**Identification:** ☐ I.D Card ☐ Credible Witness ☐ Drivers License ☐ Known Personally ☐ Passport ☐ Other:	**I.D. Number:**	
		Issued By:	
		Issued Date:	**Expiration Date:**
Document Type:	**Date/Time Notarized:** AM PM	**Document Date:**	**Fee Charged:**

Printed Name and Address of Witness:	**Phone Number:**
	Email:
	Witness' Signature:
Comments :	**Record Number:**

NOTARY RECORD

Printed Name and Address of Signer:	**Phone Number:**	**Thumb Print:**
	Email:	
	Signer's Signature:	

Service Performed: ☐ Oath ☐ Acknowledgment ☐ Jurat ☐ Other:	**Identification:** ☐ I.D Card ☐ Credible Witness ☐ Drivers License ☐ Known Personally ☐ Passport ☐ Other:	**I.D. Number:**	
		Issued By:	
		Issued Date:	**Expiration Date:**
Document Type:	**Date/Time Notarized:** AM PM	**Document Date:**	**Fee Charged:**

Printed Name and Address of Witness:	**Phone Number:**
	Email:
	Witness' Signature:
Comments :	**Record Number:**

NOTARY RECORD

Printed Name and Address of Signer:

Phone Number:

Email:

Signer's Signature:

Thumb Print:

Service Performed:

- ☐ Oath
- ☐ Acknowledgment
- ☐ Jurat
- ☐ Other:

Identification:

- ☐ I.D Card
- ☐ Credible Witness
- ☐ Drivers License
- ☐ Known Personally
- ☐ Passport
- ☐ Other:

I.D. Number:

Issued By:

Issued Date:

Expiration Date:

Document Type:

Date/Time Notarized: **AM** **PM**

Document Date:

Fee Charged:

Printed Name and Address of Witness:

Phone Number:

Email:

Witness' Signature:

Comments :

Record Number:

NOTARY RECORD

Printed Name and Address of Signer:

Phone Number:

Email:

Signer's Signature:

Thumb Print:

Service Performed:

- ☐ Oath
- ☐ Acknowledgment
- ☐ Jurat
- ☐ Other:

Identification:

- ☐ I.D Card
- ☐ Credible Witness
- ☐ Drivers License
- ☐ Known Personally
- ☐ Passport
- ☐ Other:

I.D. Number:

Issued By:

Issued Date:

Expiration Date:

Document Type:

Date/Time Notarized: **AM** **PM**

Document Date:

Fee Charged:

Printed Name and Address of Witness:

Phone Number:

Email:

Witness' Signature:

Comments :

Record Number:

NOTARY RECORD

Printed Name and Address of Signer:

Phone Number:

Email:

Signer's Signature:

Thumb Print:

Service Performed:
- ☐ Oath
- ☐ Acknowledgment
- ☐ Jurat
- ☐ Other:

Identification:
- ☐ I.D Card
- ☐ Credible Witness
- ☐ Drivers License
- ☐ Known Personally
- ☐ Passport
- ☐ Other:

I.D. Number:

Issued By:

Issued Date:

Expiration Date:

Document Type:

Date/Time Notarized: AM PM

Document Date:

Fee Charged:

Printed Name and Address of Witness:

Phone Number:

Email:

Witness' Signature:

Comments :

Record Number:

NOTARY RECORD

Printed Name and Address of Signer:

Phone Number:

Email:

Signer's Signature:

Thumb Print:

Service Performed:
- ☐ Oath
- ☐ Acknowledgment
- ☐ Jurat
- ☐ Other:

Identification:
- ☐ I.D Card
- ☐ Credible Witness
- ☐ Drivers License
- ☐ Known Personally
- ☐ Passport
- ☐ Other:

I.D. Number:

Issued By:

Issued Date:

Expiration Date:

Document Type:

Date/Time Notarized: AM PM

Document Date:

Fee Charged:

Printed Name and Address of Witness:

Phone Number:

Email:

Witness' Signature:

Comments :

Record Number:

NOTARY RECORD

Printed Name and Address of Signer:	Phone Number:	Thumb Print:
	Email:	
	Signer's Signature:	

Service Performed:	Identification:		I.D. Number:	
☐ Oath	☐ I.D Card	☐ Credible Witness	Issued By:	
☐ Acknowledgment	☐ Drivers License	☐ Known Personally		
☐ Jurat	☐ Passport		Issued Date:	Expiration Date:
☐ Other:	☐ Other:			
Document Type:	Date/Time Notarized: AM PM		Document Date:	Fee Charged:

Printed Name and Address of Witness:	Phone Number:
	Email:
	Witness' Signature:

Comments :	Record Number:

NOTARY RECORD

Printed Name and Address of Signer:	Phone Number:	Thumb Print:
	Email:	
	Signer's Signature:	

Service Performed:	Identification:		I.D. Number:	
☐ Oath	☐ I.D Card	☐ Credible Witness	Issued By:	
☐ Acknowledgment	☐ Drivers License	☐ Known Personally		
☐ Jurat	☐ Passport		Issued Date:	Expiration Date:
☐ Other:	☐ Other:			
Document Type:	Date/Time Notarized: AM PM		Document Date:	Fee Charged:

Printed Name and Address of Witness:	Phone Number:
	Email:
	Witness' Signature:

Comments :	Record Number:

NOTARY RECORD

Printed Name and Address of Signer:	**Phone Number:**	**Thumb Print:**
	Email:	
	Signer's Signature:	

Service Performed: ☐ Oath ☐ Acknowledgment ☐ Jurat ☐ Other:	**Identification:** ☐ I.D Card ☐ Credible Witness ☐ Drivers License ☐ Known Personally ☐ Passport ☐ Other:	**I.D. Number:**	
		Issued By:	
		Issued Date:	**Expiration Date:**
Document Type:	**Date/Time Notarized:** AM PM	**Document Date:**	**Fee Charged:**

Printed Name and Address of Witness:	**Phone Number:**
	Email:
	Witness' Signature:
Comments :	**Record Number:**

NOTARY RECORD

Printed Name and Address of Signer:	**Phone Number:**	**Thumb Print:**
	Email:	
	Signer's Signature:	

Service Performed: ☐ Oath ☐ Acknowledgment ☐ Jurat ☐ Other:	**Identification:** ☐ I.D Card ☐ Credible Witness ☐ Drivers License ☐ Known Personally ☐ Passport ☐ Other:	**I.D. Number:**	
		Issued By:	
		Issued Date:	**Expiration Date:**
Document Type:	**Date/Time Notarized:** AM PM	**Document Date:**	**Fee Charged:**

Printed Name and Address of Witness:	**Phone Number:**
	Email:
	Witness' Signature:
Comments :	**Record Number:**

NOTARY RECORD

Printed Name and Address of Signer:

Phone Number:

Email:

Signer's Signature:

Thumb Print:

Service Performed:

- ☐ Oath
- ☐ Acknowledgment
- ☐ Jurat
- ☐ Other:

Identification:

- ☐ I.D Card
- ☐ Credible Witness
- ☐ Drivers License
- ☐ Known Personally
- ☐ Passport
- ☐ Other:

I.D. Number:

Issued By:

Issued Date:

Expiration Date:

Document Type:

Date/Time Notarized: **AM** **PM**

Document Date:

Fee Charged:

Printed Name and Address of Witness:

Phone Number:

Email:

Witness' Signature:

Comments :

Record Number:

NOTARY RECORD

Printed Name and Address of Signer:

Phone Number:

Email:

Signer's Signature:

Thumb Print:

Service Performed:

- ☐ Oath
- ☐ Acknowledgment
- ☐ Jurat
- ☐ Other:

Identification:

- ☐ I.D Card
- ☐ Credible Witness
- ☐ Drivers License
- ☐ Known Personally
- ☐ Passport
- ☐ Other:

I.D. Number:

Issued By:

Issued Date:

Expiration Date:

Document Type:

Date/Time Notarized: **AM** **PM**

Document Date:

Fee Charged:

Printed Name and Address of Witness:

Phone Number:

Email:

Witness' Signature:

Comments :

Record Number:

NOTARY RECORD

Printed Name and Address of Signer:	**Phone Number:**	**Thumb Print:**
	Email:	
	Signer's Signature:	

Service Performed: ☐ Oath ☐ Acknowledgment ☐ Jurat ☐ Other:	**Identification:** ☐ I.D Card ☐ Credible Witness ☐ Drivers License ☐ Known Personally ☐ Passport ☐ Other:	**I.D. Number:**	
		Issued By:	
		Issued Date:	**Expiration Date:**
Document Type:	**Date/Time Notarized:** AM PM	**Document Date:**	**Fee Charged:**

Printed Name and Address of Witness:	**Phone Number:**
	Email:
	Witness' Signature:

Comments :	**Record Number:**

NOTARY RECORD

Printed Name and Address of Signer:	**Phone Number:**	**Thumb Print:**
	Email:	
	Signer's Signature:	

Service Performed: ☐ Oath ☐ Acknowledgment ☐ Jurat ☐ Other:	**Identification:** ☐ I.D Card ☐ Credible Witness ☐ Drivers License ☐ Known Personally ☐ Passport ☐ Other:	**I.D. Number:**	
		Issued By:	
		Issued Date:	**Expiration Date:**
Document Type:	**Date/Time Notarized:** AM PM	**Document Date:**	**Fee Charged:**

Printed Name and Address of Witness:	**Phone Number:**
	Email:
	Witness' Signature:

Comments :	**Record Number:**

NOTARY RECORD

Printed Name and Address of Signer:	Phone Number:	Thumb Print:
	Email:	
	Signer's Signature:	

Service Performed:	Identification:		I.D. Number:	
☐ Oath	☐ I.D Card	☐ Credible Witness	Issued By:	
☐ Acknowledgment	☐ Drivers License	☐ Known Personally	Issued Date:	Expiration Date:
☐ Jurat	☐ Passport			
☐ Other:	☐ Other:			
Document Type:	Date/Time Notarized: AM PM		Document Date:	Fee Charged:

Printed Name and Address of Witness:	Phone Number:
	Email:
	Witness' Signature:

Comments :	Record Number:

NOTARY RECORD

Printed Name and Address of Signer:	Phone Number:	Thumb Print:
	Email:	
	Signer's Signature:	

Service Performed:	Identification:		I.D. Number:	
☐ Oath	☐ I.D Card	☐ Credible Witness	Issued By:	
☐ Acknowledgment	☐ Drivers License	☐ Known Personally	Issued Date:	Expiration Date:
☐ Jurat	☐ Passport			
☐ Other:	☐ Other:			
Document Type:	Date/Time Notarized: AM PM		Document Date:	Fee Charged:

Printed Name and Address of Witness:	Phone Number:
	Email:
	Witness' Signature:

Comments :	Record Number:

NOTARY RECORD

Printed Name and Address of Signer:

Phone Number:

Email:

Signer's Signature:

Thumb Print:

Service Performed:

- ☐ Oath
- ☐ Acknowledgment
- ☐ Jurat
- ☐ Other:

Identification:

- ☐ I.D Card
- ☐ Credible Witness
- ☐ Drivers License
- ☐ Known Personally
- ☐ Passport
- ☐ Other:

I.D. Number:

Issued By:

Issued Date:

Expiration Date:

Document Type:

Date/Time Notarized: **AM** **PM**

Document Date:

Fee Charged:

Printed Name and Address of Witness:

Phone Number:

Email:

Witness' Signature:

Comments :

Record Number:

NOTARY RECORD

Printed Name and Address of Signer:

Phone Number:

Email:

Signer's Signature:

Thumb Print:

Service Performed:

- ☐ Oath
- ☐ Acknowledgment
- ☐ Jurat
- ☐ Other:

Identification:

- ☐ I.D Card
- ☐ Credible Witness
- ☐ Drivers License
- ☐ Known Personally
- ☐ Passport
- ☐ Other:

I.D. Number:

Issued By:

Issued Date:

Expiration Date:

Document Type:

Date/Time Notarized: **AM** **PM**

Document Date:

Fee Charged:

Printed Name and Address of Witness:

Phone Number:

Email:

Witness' Signature:

Comments :

Record Number:

NOTARY RECORD

Printed Name and Address of Signer:	**Phone Number:**	**Thumb Print:**
	Email:	
	Signer's Signature:	

Service Performed: ☐ Oath ☐ Acknowledgment ☐ Jurat ☐ Other:	**Identification:** ☐ I.D Card ☐ Credible Witness ☐ Drivers License ☐ Known Personally ☐ Passport ☐ Other:	**I.D. Number:**	
		Issued By:	
		Issued Date:	**Expiration Date:**
Document Type:	**Date/Time Notarized:** **AM PM**	**Document Date:**	**Fee Charged:**

Printed Name and Address of Witness:	**Phone Number:**
	Email:
	Witness' Signature:
Comments :	**Record Number:**

NOTARY RECORD

Printed Name and Address of Signer:	**Phone Number:**	**Thumb Print:**
	Email:	
	Signer's Signature:	

Service Performed: ☐ Oath ☐ Acknowledgment ☐ Jurat ☐ Other:	**Identification:** ☐ I.D Card ☐ Credible Witness ☐ Drivers License ☐ Known Personally ☐ Passport ☐ Other:	**I.D. Number:**	
		Issued By:	
		Issued Date:	**Expiration Date:**
Document Type:	**Date/Time Notarized:** **AM PM**	**Document Date:**	**Fee Charged:**

Printed Name and Address of Witness:	**Phone Number:**
	Email:
	Witness' Signature:
Comments :	**Record Number:**

NOTARY RECORD

Printed Name and Address of Signer:	Phone Number:	Thumb Print:
	Email:	
	Signer's Signature:	

Service Performed:	Identification:		I.D. Number:	
☐ Oath	☐ I.D Card	☐ Credible Witness	Issued By:	
☐ Acknowledgment	☐ Drivers License	☐ Known Personally	Issued Date:	Expiration Date:
☐ Jurat	☐ Passport			
☐ Other:	☐ Other:			
Document Type:	Date/Time Notarized: AM PM		Document Date:	Fee Charged:

Printed Name and Address of Witness:	Phone Number:
	Email:
	Witness' Signature:

Comments :	Record Number:

NOTARY RECORD

Printed Name and Address of Signer:	Phone Number:	Thumb Print:
	Email:	
	Signer's Signature:	

Service Performed:	Identification:		I.D. Number:	
☐ Oath	☐ I.D Card	☐ Credible Witness	Issued By:	
☐ Acknowledgment	☐ Drivers License	☐ Known Personally	Issued Date:	Expiration Date:
☐ Jurat	☐ Passport			
☐ Other:	☐ Other:			
Document Type:	Date/Time Notarized: AM PM		Document Date:	Fee Charged:

Printed Name and Address of Witness:	Phone Number:
	Email:
	Witness' Signature:

Comments :	Record Number:

NOTARY RECORD

Printed Name and Address of Signer:	Phone Number:	Thumb Print:
	Email:	
	Signer's Signature:	

Service Performed:	Identification:		I.D. Number:	
☐ Oath	☐ I.D Card	☐ Credible Witness		
☐ Acknowledgment	☐ Drivers License	☐ Known Personally	Issued By:	
☐ Jurat	☐ Passport			
☐ Other:	☐ Other:		Issued Date:	Expiration Date:
Document Type:	Date/Time Notarized:	AM PM	Document Date:	Fee Charged:

Printed Name and Address of Witness:	Phone Number:
	Email:
	Witness' Signature:

Comments :	Record Number:

NOTARY RECORD

Printed Name and Address of Signer:	Phone Number:	Thumb Print:
	Email:	
	Signer's Signature:	

Service Performed:	Identification:		I.D. Number:	
☐ Oath	☐ I.D Card	☐ Credible Witness		
☐ Acknowledgment	☐ Drivers License	☐ Known Personally	Issued By:	
☐ Jurat	☐ Passport			
☐ Other:	☐ Other:		Issued Date:	Expiration Date:
Document Type:	Date/Time Notarized:	AM PM	Document Date:	Fee Charged:

Printed Name and Address of Witness:	Phone Number:
	Email:
	Witness' Signature:

Comments :	Record Number:

NOTARY RECORD

Printed Name and Address of Signer:

Phone Number:

Email:

Signer's Signature:

Thumb Print:

Service Performed:

- [ ] Oath
- [ ] Acknowledgment
- [ ] Jurat
- [ ] Other:

Identification:

- [ ] I.D Card
- [ ] Credible Witness
- [ ] Drivers License
- [ ] Known Personally
- [ ] Passport
- [ ] Other:

I.D. Number:

Issued By:

Issued Date:

Expiration Date:

Document Type:

Date/Time Notarized: AM PM

Document Date:

Fee Charged:

Printed Name and Address of Witness:

Phone Number:

Email:

Witness' Signature:

Comments :

Record Number:

NOTARY RECORD

Printed Name and Address of Signer:

Phone Number:

Email:

Signer's Signature:

Thumb Print:

Service Performed:

- [ ] Oath
- [ ] Acknowledgment
- [ ] Jurat
- [ ] Other:

Identification:

- [ ] I.D Card
- [ ] Credible Witness
- [ ] Drivers License
- [ ] Known Personally
- [ ] Passport
- [ ] Other:

I.D. Number:

Issued By:

Issued Date:

Expiration Date:

Document Type:

Date/Time Notarized: AM PM

Document Date:

Fee Charged:

Printed Name and Address of Witness:

Phone Number:

Email:

Witness' Signature:

Comments :

Record Number:

NOTARY RECORD

Printed Name and Address of Signer:

Phone Number:

Email:

Signer's Signature:

Thumb Print:

Service Performed:
- ☐ Oath
- ☐ Acknowledgment
- ☐ Jurat
- ☐ Other:

Identification:
- ☐ I.D Card
- ☐ Credible Witness
- ☐ Drivers License
- ☐ Known Personally
- ☐ Passport
- ☐ Other:

I.D. Number:

Issued By:

Issued Date:

Expiration Date:

Document Type:

Date/Time Notarized: **AM** **PM**

Document Date:

Fee Charged:

Printed Name and Address of Witness:

Phone Number:

Email:

Witness' Signature:

Comments :

Record Number:

NOTARY RECORD

Printed Name and Address of Signer:

Phone Number:

Email:

Signer's Signature:

Thumb Print:

Service Performed:
- ☐ Oath
- ☐ Acknowledgment
- ☐ Jurat
- ☐ Other:

Identification:
- ☐ I.D Card
- ☐ Credible Witness
- ☐ Drivers License
- ☐ Known Personally
- ☐ Passport
- ☐ Other:

I.D. Number:

Issued By:

Issued Date:

Expiration Date:

Document Type:

Date/Time Notarized: **AM** **PM**

Document Date:

Fee Charged:

Printed Name and Address of Witness:

Phone Number:

Email:

Witness' Signature:

Comments :

Record Number:

NOTARY RECORD

Printed Name and Address of Signer:	Phone Number:	Thumb Print:
	Email:	
	Signer's Signature:	

Service Performed:	Identification:		I.D. Number:	
☐ Oath	☐ I.D Card	☐ Credible Witness		
☐ Acknowledgment	☐ Drivers License	☐ Known Personally	Issued By:	
☐ Jurat	☐ Passport			
☐ Other:	☐ Other:		Issued Date:	Expiration Date:
Document Type:	Date/Time Notarized: AM PM		Document Date:	Fee Charged:

Printed Name and Address of Witness:	Phone Number:
	Email:
	Witness' Signature:

Comments :	Record Number:

NOTARY RECORD

Printed Name and Address of Signer:	Phone Number:	Thumb Print:
	Email:	
	Signer's Signature:	

Service Performed:	Identification:		I.D. Number:	
☐ Oath	☐ I.D Card	☐ Credible Witness		
☐ Acknowledgment	☐ Drivers License	☐ Known Personally	Issued By:	
☐ Jurat	☐ Passport			
☐ Other:	☐ Other:		Issued Date:	Expiration Date:
Document Type:	Date/Time Notarized: AM PM		Document Date:	Fee Charged:

Printed Name and Address of Witness:	Phone Number:
	Email:
	Witness' Signature:

Comments :	Record Number:

NOTARY RECORD

Printed Name and Address of Signer:	Phone Number:	Thumb Print:
	Email:	
	Signer's Signature:	

Service Performed:	Identification:		I.D. Number:	
☐ Oath	☐ I.D Card	☐ Credible Witness	Issued By:	
☐ Acknowledgment	☐ Drivers License	☐ Known Personally		
☐ Jurat	☐ Passport		Issued Date:	Expiration Date:
☐ Other:	☐ Other:			
Document Type:	Date/Time Notarized: AM PM		Document Date:	Fee Charged:

Printed Name and Address of Witness:	Phone Number:
	Email:
	Witness' Signature:

Comments :	Record Number:

NOTARY RECORD

Printed Name and Address of Signer:	Phone Number:	Thumb Print:
	Email:	
	Signer's Signature:	

Service Performed:	Identification:		I.D. Number:	
☐ Oath	☐ I.D Card	☐ Credible Witness	Issued By:	
☐ Acknowledgment	☐ Drivers License	☐ Known Personally		
☐ Jurat	☐ Passport		Issued Date:	Expiration Date:
☐ Other:	☐ Other:			
Document Type:	Date/Time Notarized: AM PM		Document Date:	Fee Charged:

Printed Name and Address of Witness:	Phone Number:
	Email:
	Witness' Signature:

Comments :	Record Number:

NOTARY RECORD

Printed Name and Address of Signer:	Phone Number:	Thumb Print:
	Email:	
	Signer's Signature:	

Service Performed:	Identification:		I.D. Number:	
☐ Oath	☐ I.D Card	☐ Credible Witness	Issued By:	
☐ Acknowledgment	☐ Drivers License	☐ Known Personally	Issued Date:	Expiration Date:
☐ Jurat	☐ Passport			
☐ Other:	☐ Other:			
Document Type:	Date/Time Notarized: AM PM		Document Date:	Fee Charged:

Printed Name and Address of Witness:	Phone Number:
	Email:
	Witness' Signature:

Comments :	Record Number:

NOTARY RECORD

Printed Name and Address of Signer:	Phone Number:	Thumb Print:
	Email:	
	Signer's Signature:	

Service Performed:	Identification:		I.D. Number:	
☐ Oath	☐ I.D Card	☐ Credible Witness	Issued By:	
☐ Acknowledgment	☐ Drivers License	☐ Known Personally	Issued Date:	Expiration Date:
☐ Jurat	☐ Passport			
☐ Other:	☐ Other:			
Document Type:	Date/Time Notarized: AM PM		Document Date:	Fee Charged:

Printed Name and Address of Witness:	Phone Number:
	Email:
	Witness' Signature:

Comments :	Record Number:

NOTARY RECORD

Printed Name and Address of Signer:	Phone Number:	Thumb Print:
	Email:	
	Signer's Signature:	

Service Performed:	Identification:		I.D. Number:	
☐ Oath	☐ I.D Card	☐ Credible Witness		
☐ Acknowledgment	☐ Drivers License	☐ Known Personally	Issued By:	
☐ Jurat	☐ Passport			
☐ Other:	☐ Other:		Issued Date:	Expiration Date:
Document Type:	Date/Time Notarized: AM PM		Document Date:	Fee Charged:

Printed Name and Address of Witness:	Phone Number:
	Email:
	Witness' Signature:

Comments :	Record Number:

NOTARY RECORD

Printed Name and Address of Signer:	Phone Number:	Thumb Print:
	Email:	
	Signer's Signature:	

Service Performed:	Identification:		I.D. Number:	
☐ Oath	☐ I.D Card	☐ Credible Witness		
☐ Acknowledgment	☐ Drivers License	☐ Known Personally	Issued By:	
☐ Jurat	☐ Passport			
☐ Other:	☐ Other:		Issued Date:	Expiration Date:
Document Type:	Date/Time Notarized: AM PM		Document Date:	Fee Charged:

Printed Name and Address of Witness:	Phone Number:
	Email:
	Witness' Signature:

Comments :	Record Number:

NOTARY RECORD

Printed Name and Address of Signer:	**Phone Number:**	**Thumb Print:**
	Email:	
	Signer's Signature:	

Service Performed: ☐ Oath ☐ Acknowledgment ☐ Jurat ☐ Other:	**Identification:** ☐ I.D Card ☐ Credible Witness ☐ Drivers License ☐ Known Personally ☐ Passport ☐ Other:	**I.D. Number:**	
		Issued By:	
		Issued Date:	**Expiration Date:**
Document Type:	**Date/Time Notarized:** AM PM	**Document Date:**	**Fee Charged:**

Printed Name and Address of Witness:	**Phone Number:**
	Email:
	Witness' Signature:
Comments :	**Record Number:**

NOTARY RECORD

Printed Name and Address of Signer:	**Phone Number:**	**Thumb Print:**
	Email:	
	Signer's Signature:	

Service Performed: ☐ Oath ☐ Acknowledgment ☐ Jurat ☐ Other:	**Identification:** ☐ I.D Card ☐ Credible Witness ☐ Drivers License ☐ Known Personally ☐ Passport ☐ Other:	**I.D. Number:**	
		Issued By:	
		Issued Date:	**Expiration Date:**
Document Type:	**Date/Time Notarized:** AM PM	**Document Date:**	**Fee Charged:**

Printed Name and Address of Witness:	**Phone Number:**
	Email:
	Witness' Signature:
Comments :	**Record Number:**

NOTARY RECORD

Printed Name and Address of Signer:	Phone Number:	Thumb Print:
	Email:	
	Signer's Signature:	

Service Performed:	Identification:		I.D. Number:	
☐ Oath	☐ I.D Card	☐ Credible Witness		
☐ Acknowledgment	☐ Drivers License	☐ Known Personally	Issued By:	
☐ Jurat	☐ Passport			
☐ Other:	☐ Other:		Issued Date:	Expiration Date:
Document Type:	Date/Time Notarized: AM PM		Document Date:	Fee Charged:

Printed Name and Address of Witness:	Phone Number:
	Email:
	Witness' Signature:

Comments :	Record Number:

NOTARY RECORD

Printed Name and Address of Signer:	Phone Number:	Thumb Print:
	Email:	
	Signer's Signature:	

Service Performed:	Identification:		I.D. Number:	
☐ Oath	☐ I.D Card	☐ Credible Witness		
☐ Acknowledgment	☐ Drivers License	☐ Known Personally	Issued By:	
☐ Jurat	☐ Passport			
☐ Other:	☐ Other:		Issued Date:	Expiration Date:
Document Type:	Date/Time Notarized: AM PM		Document Date:	Fee Charged:

Printed Name and Address of Witness:	Phone Number:
	Email:
	Witness' Signature:

Comments :	Record Number:

NOTARY RECORD

Printed Name and Address of Signer:	**Phone Number:**	**Thumb Print:**
	Email:	
	Signer's Signature:	

Service Performed: ☐ Oath ☐ Acknowledgment ☐ Jurat ☐ Other:	**Identification:** ☐ I.D Card ☐ Credible Witness ☐ Drivers License ☐ Known Personally ☐ Passport ☐ Other:	**I.D. Number:**	
		Issued By:	
		Issued Date:	**Expiration Date:**
Document Type:	**Date/Time Notarized:** AM PM	**Document Date:**	**Fee Charged:**

Printed Name and Address of Witness:	**Phone Number:**
	Email:
	Witness' Signature:
Comments :	**Record Number:**

NOTARY RECORD

Printed Name and Address of Signer:	**Phone Number:**	**Thumb Print:**
	Email:	
	Signer's Signature:	

Service Performed: ☐ Oath ☐ Acknowledgment ☐ Jurat ☐ Other:	**Identification:** ☐ I.D Card ☐ Credible Witness ☐ Drivers License ☐ Known Personally ☐ Passport ☐ Other:	**I.D. Number:**	
		Issued By:	
		Issued Date:	**Expiration Date:**
Document Type:	**Date/Time Notarized:** AM PM	**Document Date:**	**Fee Charged:**

Printed Name and Address of Witness:	**Phone Number:**
	Email:
	Witness' Signature:
Comments :	**Record Number:**

NOTARY RECORD

Printed Name and Address of Signer:

Phone Number:

Email:

Signer's Signature:

Thumb Print:

Service Performed:
- ☐ Oath
- ☐ Acknowledgment
- ☐ Jurat
- ☐ Other:

Identification:
- ☐ I.D Card
- ☐ Credible Witness
- ☐ Drivers License
- ☐ Known Personally
- ☐ Passport
- ☐ Other:

I.D. Number:

Issued By:

Issued Date:

Expiration Date:

Document Type:

Date/Time Notarized: **AM** **PM**

Document Date:

Fee Charged:

Printed Name and Address of Witness:

Phone Number:

Email:

Witness' Signature:

Comments :

Record Number:

NOTARY RECORD

Printed Name and Address of Signer:

Phone Number:

Email:

Signer's Signature:

Thumb Print:

Service Performed:
- ☐ Oath
- ☐ Acknowledgment
- ☐ Jurat
- ☐ Other:

Identification:
- ☐ I.D Card
- ☐ Credible Witness
- ☐ Drivers License
- ☐ Known Personally
- ☐ Passport
- ☐ Other:

I.D. Number:

Issued By:

Issued Date:

Expiration Date:

Document Type:

Date/Time Notarized: **AM** **PM**

Document Date:

Fee Charged:

Printed Name and Address of Witness:

Phone Number:

Email:

Witness' Signature:

Comments :

Record Number:

NOTARY RECORD

Printed Name and Address of Signer:	Phone Number:	Thumb Print:
	Email:	
	Signer's Signature:	

Service Performed:	Identification:	I.D. Number:	
☐ Oath ☐ Acknowledgment ☐ Jurat ☐ Other:	☐ I.D Card ☐ Credible Witness ☐ Drivers License ☐ Known Personally ☐ Passport ☐ Other:	Issued By:	
		Issued Date:	Expiration Date:
Document Type:	Date/Time Notarized: AM PM	Document Date:	Fee Charged:

Printed Name and Address of Witness:	Phone Number:
	Email:
	Witness' Signature:

Comments :	Record Number:

NOTARY RECORD

Printed Name and Address of Signer:	Phone Number:	Thumb Print:
	Email:	
	Signer's Signature:	

Service Performed:	Identification:	I.D. Number:	
☐ Oath ☐ Acknowledgment ☐ Jurat ☐ Other:	☐ I.D Card ☐ Credible Witness ☐ Drivers License ☐ Known Personally ☐ Passport ☐ Other:	Issued By:	
		Issued Date:	Expiration Date:
Document Type:	Date/Time Notarized: AM PM	Document Date:	Fee Charged:

Printed Name and Address of Witness:	Phone Number:
	Email:
	Witness' Signature:

Comments :	Record Number:

NOTARY RECORD

Printed Name and Address of Signer:

Phone Number:

Email:

Signer's Signature:

Thumb Print:

Service Performed:

- [ ] Oath
- [ ] Acknowledgment
- [ ] Jurat
- [ ] Other:

Identification:

- [ ] I.D Card
- [ ] Credible Witness
- [ ] Drivers License
- [ ] Known Personally
- [ ] Passport
- [ ] Other:

I.D. Number:

Issued By:

Issued Date:

Expiration Date:

Document Type:

Date/Time Notarized: **AM** **PM**

Document Date:

Fee Charged:

Printed Name and Address of Witness:

Phone Number:

Email:

Witness' Signature:

Comments :

Record Number:

NOTARY RECORD

Printed Name and Address of Signer:

Phone Number:

Email:

Signer's Signature:

Thumb Print:

Service Performed:

- [ ] Oath
- [ ] Acknowledgment
- [ ] Jurat
- [ ] Other:

Identification:

- [ ] I.D Card
- [ ] Credible Witness
- [ ] Drivers License
- [ ] Known Personally
- [ ] Passport
- [ ] Other:

I.D. Number:

Issued By:

Issued Date:

Expiration Date:

Document Type:

Date/Time Notarized: **AM** **PM**

Document Date:

Fee Charged:

Printed Name and Address of Witness:

Phone Number:

Email:

Witness' Signature:

Comments :

Record Number:

NOTARY RECORD

Printed Name and Address of Signer:	Phone Number:	Thumb Print:
	Email:	
	Signer's Signature:	

Service Performed:
- ☐ Oath
- ☐ Acknowledgment
- ☐ Jurat
- ☐ Other:

Identification:
- ☐ I.D Card
- ☐ Credible Witness
- ☐ Drivers License
- ☐ Known Personally
- ☐ Passport
- ☐ Other:

I.D. Number:	
Issued By:	
Issued Date:	Expiration Date:

Document Type:	Date/Time Notarized: AM PM	Document Date:	Fee Charged:

Printed Name and Address of Witness:	Phone Number:
	Email:
	Witness' Signature:

Comments :	Record Number:

NOTARY RECORD

Printed Name and Address of Signer:	Phone Number:	Thumb Print:
	Email:	
	Signer's Signature:	

Service Performed:
- ☐ Oath
- ☐ Acknowledgment
- ☐ Jurat
- ☐ Other:

Identification:
- ☐ I.D Card
- ☐ Credible Witness
- ☐ Drivers License
- ☐ Known Personally
- ☐ Passport
- ☐ Other:

I.D. Number:	
Issued By:	
Issued Date:	Expiration Date:

Document Type:	Date/Time Notarized: AM PM	Document Date:	Fee Charged:

Printed Name and Address of Witness:	Phone Number:
	Email:
	Witness' Signature:

Comments :	Record Number:

NOTARY RECORD

Printed Name and Address of Signer:

Phone Number:

Email:

Signer's Signature:

Thumb Print:

Service Performed:

- ☐ Oath
- ☐ Acknowledgment
- ☐ Jurat
- ☐ Other:

Identification:

- ☐ I.D Card
- ☐ Credible Witness
- ☐ Drivers License
- ☐ Known Personally
- ☐ Passport
- ☐ Other:

I.D. Number:

Issued By:

Issued Date:

Expiration Date:

Document Type:

Date/Time Notarized: **AM** **PM**

Document Date:

Fee Charged:

Printed Name and Address of Witness:

Phone Number:

Email:

Witness' Signature:

Comments :

Record Number:

NOTARY RECORD

Printed Name and Address of Signer:

Phone Number:

Email:

Signer's Signature:

Thumb Print:

Service Performed:

- ☐ Oath
- ☐ Acknowledgment
- ☐ Jurat
- ☐ Other:

Identification:

- ☐ I.D Card
- ☐ Credible Witness
- ☐ Drivers License
- ☐ Known Personally
- ☐ Passport
- ☐ Other:

I.D. Number:

Issued By:

Issued Date:

Expiration Date:

Document Type:

Date/Time Notarized: **AM** **PM**

Document Date:

Fee Charged:

Printed Name and Address of Witness:

Phone Number:

Email:

Witness' Signature:

Comments :

Record Number:

NOTARY RECORD

Printed Name and Address of Signer:	**Phone Number:**	**Thumb Print:**
	Email:	
	Signer's Signature:	

Service Performed: ☐ Oath ☐ Acknowledgment ☐ Jurat ☐ Other:	**Identification:** ☐ I.D Card ☐ Credible Witness ☐ Drivers License ☐ Known Personally ☐ Passport ☐ Other:	**I.D. Number:**	
		Issued By:	
		Issued Date:	**Expiration Date:**
Document Type:	**Date/Time Notarized:** AM PM	**Document Date:**	**Fee Charged:**

Printed Name and Address of Witness:	**Phone Number:**
	Email:
	Witness' Signature:
Comments :	**Record Number:**

NOTARY RECORD

Printed Name and Address of Signer:	**Phone Number:**	**Thumb Print:**
	Email:	
	Signer's Signature:	

Service Performed: ☐ Oath ☐ Acknowledgment ☐ Jurat ☐ Other:	**Identification:** ☐ I.D Card ☐ Credible Witness ☐ Drivers License ☐ Known Personally ☐ Passport ☐ Other:	**I.D. Number:**	
		Issued By:	
		Issued Date:	**Expiration Date:**
Document Type:	**Date/Time Notarized:** AM PM	**Document Date:**	**Fee Charged:**

Printed Name and Address of Witness:	**Phone Number:**
	Email:
	Witness' Signature:
Comments :	**Record Number:**

NOTARY RECORD

Printed Name and Address of Signer:	Phone Number:	Thumb Print:
	Email:	
	Signer's Signature:	

Service Performed:	Identification:		I.D. Number:	
☐ Oath	☐ I.D Card	☐ Credible Witness	Issued By:	
☐ Acknowledgment	☐ Drivers License	☐ Known Personally		
☐ Jurat	☐ Passport		Issued Date:	Expiration Date:
☐ Other:	☐ Other:			
Document Type:	Date/Time Notarized:	AM PM	Document Date:	Fee Charged:

Printed Name and Address of Witness:	Phone Number:
	Email:
	Witness' Signature:

Comments :	Record Number:

NOTARY RECORD

Printed Name and Address of Signer:	Phone Number:	Thumb Print:
	Email:	
	Signer's Signature:	

Service Performed:	Identification:		I.D. Number:	
☐ Oath	☐ I.D Card	☐ Credible Witness	Issued By:	
☐ Acknowledgment	☐ Drivers License	☐ Known Personally		
☐ Jurat	☐ Passport		Issued Date:	Expiration Date:
☐ Other:	☐ Other:			
Document Type:	Date/Time Notarized:	AM PM	Document Date:	Fee Charged:

Printed Name and Address of Witness:	Phone Number:
	Email:
	Witness' Signature:

Comments :	Record Number:

NOTARY RECORD

Printed Name and Address of Signer:	**Phone Number:**	**Thumb Print:**
	Email:	
	Signer's Signature:	

Service Performed: ☐ Oath ☐ Acknowledgment ☐ Jurat ☐ Other:	**Identification:** ☐ I.D Card ☐ Credible Witness ☐ Drivers License ☐ Known Personally ☐ Passport ☐ Other:	**I.D. Number:**	
		Issued By:	
		Issued Date:	**Expiration Date:**
Document Type:	**Date/Time Notarized:** AM PM	**Document Date:**	**Fee Charged:**

Printed Name and Address of Witness:	**Phone Number:**
	Email:
	Witness' Signature:

Comments :	**Record Number:**

NOTARY RECORD

Printed Name and Address of Signer:	**Phone Number:**	**Thumb Print:**
	Email:	
	Signer's Signature:	

Service Performed: ☐ Oath ☐ Acknowledgment ☐ Jurat ☐ Other:	**Identification:** ☐ I.D Card ☐ Credible Witness ☐ Drivers License ☐ Known Personally ☐ Passport ☐ Other:	**I.D. Number:**	
		Issued By:	
		Issued Date:	**Expiration Date:**
Document Type:	**Date/Time Notarized:** AM PM	**Document Date:**	**Fee Charged:**

Printed Name and Address of Witness:	**Phone Number:**
	Email:
	Witness' Signature:

Comments :	**Record Number:**

NOTARY RECORD

Printed Name and Address of Signer:	**Phone Number:**	**Thumb Print:**
	Email:	
	Signer's Signature:	

Service Performed: ☐ Oath ☐ Acknowledgment ☐ Jurat ☐ Other:	**Identification:** ☐ I.D Card ☐ Credible Witness ☐ Drivers License ☐ Known Personally ☐ Passport ☐ Other:	**I.D. Number:**	
		Issued By:	
		Issued Date:	**Expiration Date:**
Document Type:	**Date/Time Notarized:** AM PM	**Document Date:**	**Fee Charged:**

Printed Name and Address of Witness:	**Phone Number:**
	Email:
	Witness' Signature:

Comments :	**Record Number:**

NOTARY RECORD

Printed Name and Address of Signer:	**Phone Number:**	**Thumb Print:**
	Email:	
	Signer's Signature:	

Service Performed: ☐ Oath ☐ Acknowledgment ☐ Jurat ☐ Other:	**Identification:** ☐ I.D Card ☐ Credible Witness ☐ Drivers License ☐ Known Personally ☐ Passport ☐ Other:	**I.D. Number:**	
		Issued By:	
		Issued Date:	**Expiration Date:**
Document Type:	**Date/Time Notarized:** AM PM	**Document Date:**	**Fee Charged:**

Printed Name and Address of Witness:	**Phone Number:**
	Email:
	Witness' Signature:

Comments :	**Record Number:**

NOTARY RECORD

Printed Name and Address of Signer:	Phone Number:	Thumb Print:
	Email:	
	Signer's Signature:	

Service Performed:	Identification:		I.D. Number:	
☐ Oath	☐ I.D Card	☐ Credible Witness		
☐ Acknowledgment	☐ Drivers License	☐ Known Personally	Issued By:	
☐ Jurat	☐ Passport			
☐ Other:	☐ Other:		Issued Date:	Expiration Date:
Document Type:	Date/Time Notarized: AM PM		Document Date:	Fee Charged:

Printed Name and Address of Witness:	Phone Number:
	Email:
	Witness' Signature:

Comments :	Record Number:

NOTARY RECORD

Printed Name and Address of Signer:	Phone Number:	Thumb Print:
	Email:	
	Signer's Signature:	

Service Performed:	Identification:		I.D. Number:	
☐ Oath	☐ I.D Card	☐ Credible Witness		
☐ Acknowledgment	☐ Drivers License	☐ Known Personally	Issued By:	
☐ Jurat	☐ Passport			
☐ Other:	☐ Other:		Issued Date:	Expiration Date:
Document Type:	Date/Time Notarized: AM PM		Document Date:	Fee Charged:

Printed Name and Address of Witness:	Phone Number:
	Email:
	Witness' Signature:

Comments :	Record Number:

NOTARY RECORD

Printed Name and Address of Signer:	**Phone Number:**	**Thumb Print:**
	Email:	
	Signer's Signature:	

Service Performed: ☐ Oath ☐ Acknowledgment ☐ Jurat ☐ Other:	**Identification:** ☐ I.D Card ☐ Credible Witness ☐ Drivers License ☐ Known Personally ☐ Passport ☐ Other:	**I.D. Number:**	
		Issued By:	
		Issued Date:	**Expiration Date:**
Document Type:	**Date/Time Notarized:** AM PM	**Document Date:**	**Fee Charged:**

Printed Name and Address of Witness:	**Phone Number:**
	Email:
	Witness' Signature:

Comments :	**Record Number:**

NOTARY RECORD

Printed Name and Address of Signer:	**Phone Number:**	**Thumb Print:**
	Email:	
	Signer's Signature:	

Service Performed: ☐ Oath ☐ Acknowledgment ☐ Jurat ☐ Other:	**Identification:** ☐ I.D Card ☐ Credible Witness ☐ Drivers License ☐ Known Personally ☐ Passport ☐ Other:	**I.D. Number:**	
		Issued By:	
		Issued Date:	**Expiration Date:**
Document Type:	**Date/Time Notarized:** AM PM	**Document Date:**	**Fee Charged:**

Printed Name and Address of Witness:	**Phone Number:**
	Email:
	Witness' Signature:

Comments :	**Record Number:**

NOTARY RECORD

Printed Name and Address of Signer:

Phone Number:

Email:

Signer's Signature:

Thumb Print:

Service Performed:

- ☐ Oath
- ☐ Acknowledgment
- ☐ Jurat
- ☐ Other:

Identification:

- ☐ I.D Card
- ☐ Credible Witness
- ☐ Drivers License
- ☐ Known Personally
- ☐ Passport
- ☐ Other:

I.D. Number:

Issued By:

Issued Date:

Expiration Date:

Document Type:

Date/Time Notarized: **AM** **PM**

Document Date:

Fee Charged:

Printed Name and Address of Witness:

Phone Number:

Email:

Witness' Signature:

Comments :

Record Number:

NOTARY RECORD

Printed Name and Address of Signer:

Phone Number:

Email:

Signer's Signature:

Thumb Print:

Service Performed:

- ☐ Oath
- ☐ Acknowledgment
- ☐ Jurat
- ☐ Other:

Identification:

- ☐ I.D Card
- ☐ Credible Witness
- ☐ Drivers License
- ☐ Known Personally
- ☐ Passport
- ☐ Other:

I.D. Number:

Issued By:

Issued Date:

Expiration Date:

Document Type:

Date/Time Notarized: **AM** **PM**

Document Date:

Fee Charged:

Printed Name and Address of Witness:

Phone Number:

Email:

Witness' Signature:

Comments :

Record Number:

NOTARY RECORD

Printed Name and Address of Signer:	Phone Number:	Thumb Print:
	Email:	
	Signer's Signature:	

Service Performed:	Identification:		I.D. Number:	
☐ Oath	☐ I.D Card	☐ Credible Witness	Issued By:	
☐ Acknowledgment	☐ Drivers License	☐ Known Personally		
☐ Jurat	☐ Passport		Issued Date:	Expiration Date:
☐ Other:	☐ Other:			
Document Type:	Date/Time Notarized:	AM PM	Document Date:	Fee Charged:

Printed Name and Address of Witness:	Phone Number:
	Email:
	Witness' Signature:

Comments :	Record Number:

NOTARY RECORD

Printed Name and Address of Signer:	Phone Number:	Thumb Print:
	Email:	
	Signer's Signature:	

Service Performed:	Identification:		I.D. Number:	
☐ Oath	☐ I.D Card	☐ Credible Witness	Issued By:	
☐ Acknowledgment	☐ Drivers License	☐ Known Personally		
☐ Jurat	☐ Passport		Issued Date:	Expiration Date:
☐ Other:	☐ Other:			
Document Type:	Date/Time Notarized:	AM PM	Document Date:	Fee Charged:

Printed Name and Address of Witness:	Phone Number:
	Email:
	Witness' Signature:

Comments :	Record Number:

NOTARY RECORD

Printed Name and Address of Signer:	Phone Number:	Thumb Print:
	Email:	
	Signer's Signature:	

Service Performed:	Identification:		I.D. Number:	
☐ Oath	☐ I.D Card	☐ Credible Witness	Issued By:	
☐ Acknowledgment	☐ Drivers License	☐ Known Personally		
☐ Jurat	☐ Passport		Issued Date:	Expiration Date:
☐ Other:	☐ Other:			
Document Type:	Date/Time Notarized: AM PM		Document Date:	Fee Charged:

Printed Name and Address of Witness:	Phone Number:
	Email:
	Witness' Signature:

Comments :	Record Number:

NOTARY RECORD

Printed Name and Address of Signer:	Phone Number:	Thumb Print:
	Email:	
	Signer's Signature:	

Service Performed:	Identification:		I.D. Number:	
☐ Oath	☐ I.D Card	☐ Credible Witness	Issued By:	
☐ Acknowledgment	☐ Drivers License	☐ Known Personally		
☐ Jurat	☐ Passport		Issued Date:	Expiration Date:
☐ Other:	☐ Other:			
Document Type:	Date/Time Notarized: AM PM		Document Date:	Fee Charged:

Printed Name and Address of Witness:	Phone Number:
	Email:
	Witness' Signature:

Comments :	Record Number:

NOTARY RECORD

Printed Name and Address of Signer:	**Phone Number:**	**Thumb Print:**
	Email:	
	Signer's Signature:	

Service Performed: ☐ Oath ☐ Acknowledgment ☐ Jurat ☐ Other:	**Identification:** ☐ I.D Card ☐ Credible Witness ☐ Drivers License ☐ Known Personally ☐ Passport ☐ Other:	**I.D. Number:**	
		Issued By:	
		Issued Date:	**Expiration Date:**
Document Type:	**Date/Time Notarized:** AM PM	**Document Date:**	**Fee Charged:**

Printed Name and Address of Witness:	**Phone Number:**
	Email:
	Witness' Signature:
Comments :	**Record Number:**

NOTARY RECORD

Printed Name and Address of Signer:	**Phone Number:**	**Thumb Print:**
	Email:	
	Signer's Signature:	

Service Performed: ☐ Oath ☐ Acknowledgment ☐ Jurat ☐ Other:	**Identification:** ☐ I.D Card ☐ Credible Witness ☐ Drivers License ☐ Known Personally ☐ Passport ☐ Other:	**I.D. Number:**	
		Issued By:	
		Issued Date:	**Expiration Date:**
Document Type:	**Date/Time Notarized:** AM PM	**Document Date:**	**Fee Charged:**

Printed Name and Address of Witness:	**Phone Number:**
	Email:
	Witness' Signature:
Comments :	**Record Number:**

NOTARY RECORD

Printed Name and Address of Signer:	**Phone Number:**	**Thumb Print:**
	Email:	
	Signer's Signature:	

Service Performed: ☐ Oath ☐ Acknowledgment ☐ Jurat ☐ Other:	**Identification:** ☐ I.D Card ☐ Credible Witness ☐ Drivers License ☐ Known Personally ☐ Passport ☐ Other:	**I.D. Number:**	
		Issued By:	
		Issued Date:	**Expiration Date:**
Document Type:	**Date/Time Notarized:** AM PM	**Document Date:**	**Fee Charged:**

Printed Name and Address of Witness:	**Phone Number:**
	Email:
	Witness' Signature:
Comments :	**Record Number:**

NOTARY RECORD

Printed Name and Address of Signer:	**Phone Number:**	**Thumb Print:**
	Email:	
	Signer's Signature:	

Service Performed: ☐ Oath ☐ Acknowledgment ☐ Jurat ☐ Other:	**Identification:** ☐ I.D Card ☐ Credible Witness ☐ Drivers License ☐ Known Personally ☐ Passport ☐ Other:	**I.D. Number:**	
		Issued By:	
		Issued Date:	**Expiration Date:**
Document Type:	**Date/Time Notarized:** AM PM	**Document Date:**	**Fee Charged:**

Printed Name and Address of Witness:	**Phone Number:**
	Email:
	Witness' Signature:
Comments :	**Record Number:**

NOTARY RECORD

Printed Name and Address of Signer:	Phone Number:	Thumb Print:
	Email:	
	Signer's Signature:	

Service Performed:	Identification:		I.D. Number:	
☐ Oath	☐ I.D Card	☐ Credible Witness	Issued By:	
☐ Acknowledgment	☐ Drivers License	☐ Known Personally	Issued Date:	Expiration Date:
☐ Jurat	☐ Passport			
☐ Other:	☐ Other:			
Document Type:	Date/Time Notarized: AM PM		Document Date:	Fee Charged:

Printed Name and Address of Witness:	Phone Number:
	Email:
	Witness' Signature:

Comments :	Record Number:

NOTARY RECORD

Printed Name and Address of Signer:	Phone Number:	Thumb Print:
	Email:	
	Signer's Signature:	

Service Performed:	Identification:		I.D. Number:	
☐ Oath	☐ I.D Card	☐ Credible Witness	Issued By:	
☐ Acknowledgment	☐ Drivers License	☐ Known Personally	Issued Date:	Expiration Date:
☐ Jurat	☐ Passport			
☐ Other:	☐ Other:			
Document Type:	Date/Time Notarized: AM PM		Document Date:	Fee Charged:

Printed Name and Address of Witness:	Phone Number:
	Email:
	Witness' Signature:

Comments :	Record Number:

NOTARY RECORD

Printed Name and Address of Signer:

Phone Number:

Email:

Signer's Signature:

Thumb Print:

Service Performed:

- ☐ Oath
- ☐ Acknowledgment
- ☐ Jurat
- ☐ Other:

Identification:

- ☐ I.D Card
- ☐ Credible Witness
- ☐ Drivers License
- ☐ Known Personally
- ☐ Passport
- ☐ Other:

I.D. Number:

Issued By:

Issued Date:

Expiration Date:

Document Type:

Date/Time Notarized: AM PM

Document Date:

Fee Charged:

Printed Name and Address of Witness:

Phone Number:

Email:

Witness' Signature:

Comments :

Record Number:

NOTARY RECORD

Printed Name and Address of Signer:

Phone Number:

Email:

Signer's Signature:

Thumb Print:

Service Performed:

- ☐ Oath
- ☐ Acknowledgment
- ☐ Jurat
- ☐ Other:

Identification:

- ☐ I.D Card
- ☐ Credible Witness
- ☐ Drivers License
- ☐ Known Personally
- ☐ Passport
- ☐ Other:

I.D. Number:

Issued By:

Issued Date:

Expiration Date:

Document Type:

Date/Time Notarized: AM PM

Document Date:

Fee Charged:

Printed Name and Address of Witness:

Phone Number:

Email:

Witness' Signature:

Comments :

Record Number:

NOTARY RECORD

Printed Name and Address of Signer:	Phone Number:	Thumb Print:
	Email:	
	Signer's Signature:	

Service Performed:	Identification:		I.D. Number:	
☐ Oath	☐ I.D Card	☐ Credible Witness	Issued By:	
☐ Acknowledgment	☐ Drivers License	☐ Known Personally		
☐ Jurat	☐ Passport		Issued Date:	Expiration Date:
☐ Other:	☐ Other:			
Document Type:	Date/Time Notarized: AM PM		Document Date:	Fee Charged:

Printed Name and Address of Witness:	Phone Number:
	Email:
	Witness' Signature:

Comments :	Record Number:

NOTARY RECORD

Printed Name and Address of Signer:	Phone Number:	Thumb Print:
	Email:	
	Signer's Signature:	

Service Performed:	Identification:		I.D. Number:	
☐ Oath	☐ I.D Card	☐ Credible Witness	Issued By:	
☐ Acknowledgment	☐ Drivers License	☐ Known Personally		
☐ Jurat	☐ Passport		Issued Date:	Expiration Date:
☐ Other:	☐ Other:			
Document Type:	Date/Time Notarized: AM PM		Document Date:	Fee Charged:

Printed Name and Address of Witness:	Phone Number:
	Email:
	Witness' Signature:

Comments :	Record Number:

NOTARY RECORD

Printed Name and Address of Signer:	**Phone Number:**	**Thumb Print:**
	Email:	
	Signer's Signature:	

Service Performed: ☐ Oath ☐ Acknowledgment ☐ Jurat ☐ Other:	**Identification:** ☐ I.D Card ☐ Credible Witness ☐ Drivers License ☐ Known Personally ☐ Passport ☐ Other:	**I.D. Number:**	
		Issued By:	
		Issued Date:	**Expiration Date:**
Document Type:	**Date/Time Notarized:** AM PM	**Document Date:**	**Fee Charged:**

Printed Name and Address of Witness:	**Phone Number:**
	Email:
	Witness' Signature:
Comments :	**Record Number:**

NOTARY RECORD

Printed Name and Address of Signer:	**Phone Number:**	**Thumb Print:**
	Email:	
	Signer's Signature:	

Service Performed: ☐ Oath ☐ Acknowledgment ☐ Jurat ☐ Other:	**Identification:** ☐ I.D Card ☐ Credible Witness ☐ Drivers License ☐ Known Personally ☐ Passport ☐ Other:	**I.D. Number:**	
		Issued By:	
		Issued Date:	**Expiration Date:**
Document Type:	**Date/Time Notarized:** AM PM	**Document Date:**	**Fee Charged:**

Printed Name and Address of Witness:	**Phone Number:**
	Email:
	Witness' Signature:
Comments :	**Record Number:**

NOTARY RECORD

Printed Name and Address of Signer:	Phone Number:	Thumb Print:
	Email:	
	Signer's Signature:	

Service Performed:	Identification:		I.D. Number:	
☐ Oath	☐ I.D Card	☐ Credible Witness	Issued By:	
☐ Acknowledgment	☐ Drivers License	☐ Known Personally		
☐ Jurat	☐ Passport		Issued Date:	Expiration Date:
☐ Other:	☐ Other:			
Document Type:	Date/Time Notarized:	AM PM	Document Date:	Fee Charged:

Printed Name and Address of Witness:	Phone Number:
	Email:
	Witness' Signature:

Comments :	Record Number:

NOTARY RECORD

Printed Name and Address of Signer:	Phone Number:	Thumb Print:
	Email:	
	Signer's Signature:	

Service Performed:	Identification:		I.D. Number:	
☐ Oath	☐ I.D Card	☐ Credible Witness	Issued By:	
☐ Acknowledgment	☐ Drivers License	☐ Known Personally		
☐ Jurat	☐ Passport		Issued Date:	Expiration Date:
☐ Other:	☐ Other:			
Document Type:	Date/Time Notarized:	AM PM	Document Date:	Fee Charged:

Printed Name and Address of Witness:	Phone Number:
	Email:
	Witness' Signature:

Comments :	Record Number:

NOTARY RECORD

Printed Name and Address of Signer:	Phone Number:	Thumb Print:
	Email:	
	Signer's Signature:	

Service Performed:	Identification:		I.D. Number:	
☐ Oath	☐ I.D Card	☐ Credible Witness	Issued By:	
☐ Acknowledgment	☐ Drivers License	☐ Known Personally	Issued Date:	Expiration Date:
☐ Jurat	☐ Passport			
☐ Other:	☐ Other:			
Document Type:	Date/Time Notarized:	AM PM	Document Date:	Fee Charged:

Printed Name and Address of Witness:	Phone Number:
	Email:
	Witness' Signature:

Comments :	Record Number:

NOTARY RECORD

Printed Name and Address of Signer:	Phone Number:	Thumb Print:
	Email:	
	Signer's Signature:	

Service Performed:	Identification:		I.D. Number:	
☐ Oath	☐ I.D Card	☐ Credible Witness	Issued By:	
☐ Acknowledgment	☐ Drivers License	☐ Known Personally	Issued Date:	Expiration Date:
☐ Jurat	☐ Passport			
☐ Other:	☐ Other:			
Document Type:	Date/Time Notarized:	AM PM	Document Date:	Fee Charged:

Printed Name and Address of Witness:	Phone Number:
	Email:
	Witness' Signature:

Comments :	Record Number:

NOTARY RECORD

Printed Name and Address of Signer:	Phone Number:	Thumb Print:
	Email:	
	Signer's Signature:	

Service Performed:	Identification:		I.D. Number:	
☐ Oath	☐ I.D Card	☐ Credible Witness	Issued By:	
☐ Acknowledgment	☐ Drivers License	☐ Known Personally		
☐ Jurat	☐ Passport		Issued Date:	Expiration Date:
☐ Other:	☐ Other:			
Document Type:	Date/Time Notarized: AM PM		Document Date:	Fee Charged:

Printed Name and Address of Witness:	Phone Number:
	Email:
	Witness' Signature:

Comments :	Record Number:

NOTARY RECORD

Printed Name and Address of Signer:	Phone Number:	Thumb Print:
	Email:	
	Signer's Signature:	

Service Performed:	Identification:		I.D. Number:	
☐ Oath	☐ I.D Card	☐ Credible Witness	Issued By:	
☐ Acknowledgment	☐ Drivers License	☐ Known Personally		
☐ Jurat	☐ Passport		Issued Date:	Expiration Date:
☐ Other:	☐ Other:			
Document Type:	Date/Time Notarized: AM PM		Document Date:	Fee Charged:

Printed Name and Address of Witness:	Phone Number:
	Email:
	Witness' Signature:

Comments :	Record Number:

NOTARY RECORD

Printed Name and Address of Signer:	Phone Number:	Thumb Print:
	Email:	
	Signer's Signature:	

Service Performed:	Identification:		I.D. Number:	
☐ Oath	☐ I.D Card	☐ Credible Witness	Issued By:	
☐ Acknowledgment	☐ Drivers License	☐ Known Personally	Issued Date:	Expiration Date:
☐ Jurat	☐ Passport			
☐ Other:	☐ Other:			
Document Type:	Date/Time Notarized: AM PM		Document Date:	Fee Charged:

Printed Name and Address of Witness:	Phone Number:
	Email:
	Witness' Signature:

Comments :	Record Number:

NOTARY RECORD

Printed Name and Address of Signer:	Phone Number:	Thumb Print:
	Email:	
	Signer's Signature:	

Service Performed:	Identification:		I.D. Number:	
☐ Oath	☐ I.D Card	☐ Credible Witness	Issued By:	
☐ Acknowledgment	☐ Drivers License	☐ Known Personally	Issued Date:	Expiration Date:
☐ Jurat	☐ Passport			
☐ Other:	☐ Other:			
Document Type:	Date/Time Notarized: AM PM		Document Date:	Fee Charged:

Printed Name and Address of Witness:	Phone Number:
	Email:
	Witness' Signature:

Comments :	Record Number:

NOTARY RECORD

Printed Name and Address of Signer:	**Phone Number:**	**Thumb Print:**
	Email:	
	Signer's Signature:	

Service Performed: ☐ Oath ☐ Acknowledgment ☐ Jurat ☐ Other:	**Identification:** ☐ I.D Card ☐ Credible Witness ☐ Drivers License ☐ Known Personally ☐ Passport ☐ Other:	**I.D. Number:**	
		Issued By:	
		Issued Date:	**Expiration Date:**
Document Type:	**Date/Time Notarized:** AM PM	**Document Date:**	**Fee Charged:**

Printed Name and Address of Witness:	**Phone Number:**
	Email:
	Witness' Signature:
Comments :	**Record Number:**

NOTARY RECORD

Printed Name and Address of Signer:	**Phone Number:**	**Thumb Print:**
	Email:	
	Signer's Signature:	

Service Performed: ☐ Oath ☐ Acknowledgment ☐ Jurat ☐ Other:	**Identification:** ☐ I.D Card ☐ Credible Witness ☐ Drivers License ☐ Known Personally ☐ Passport ☐ Other:	**I.D. Number:**	
		Issued By:	
		Issued Date:	**Expiration Date:**
Document Type:	**Date/Time Notarized:** AM PM	**Document Date:**	**Fee Charged:**

Printed Name and Address of Witness:	**Phone Number:**
	Email:
	Witness' Signature:
Comments :	**Record Number:**

NOTARY RECORD

Printed Name and Address of Signer:

Phone Number:

Email:

Signer's Signature:

Thumb Print:

Service Performed:

- ☐ Oath
- ☐ Acknowledgment
- ☐ Jurat
- ☐ Other:

Identification:

- ☐ I.D Card
- ☐ Credible Witness
- ☐ Drivers License
- ☐ Known Personally
- ☐ Passport
- ☐ Other:

I.D. Number:

Issued By:

Issued Date:

Expiration Date:

Document Type:

Date/Time Notarized: **AM** **PM**

Document Date:

Fee Charged:

Printed Name and Address of Witness:

Phone Number:

Email:

Witness' Signature:

Comments :

Record Number:

NOTARY RECORD

Printed Name and Address of Signer:

Phone Number:

Email:

Signer's Signature:

Thumb Print:

Service Performed:

- ☐ Oath
- ☐ Acknowledgment
- ☐ Jurat
- ☐ Other:

Identification:

- ☐ I.D Card
- ☐ Credible Witness
- ☐ Drivers License
- ☐ Known Personally
- ☐ Passport
- ☐ Other:

I.D. Number:

Issued By:

Issued Date:

Expiration Date:

Document Type:

Date/Time Notarized: **AM** **PM**

Document Date:

Fee Charged:

Printed Name and Address of Witness:

Phone Number:

Email:

Witness' Signature:

Comments :

Record Number:

NOTARY RECORD

Printed Name and Address of Signer:	**Phone Number:**	**Thumb Print:**
	Email:	
	Signer's Signature:	

Service Performed: ☐ Oath ☐ Acknowledgment ☐ Jurat ☐ Other:	**Identification:** ☐ I.D Card ☐ Credible Witness ☐ Drivers License ☐ Known Personally ☐ Passport ☐ Other:	**I.D. Number:**	
		Issued By:	
		Issued Date:	**Expiration Date:**
Document Type:	**Date/Time Notarized:** **AM PM**	**Document Date:**	**Fee Charged:**

Printed Name and Address of Witness:	**Phone Number:**
	Email:
	Witness' Signature:

Comments :	**Record Number:**

NOTARY RECORD

Printed Name and Address of Signer:	**Phone Number:**	**Thumb Print:**
	Email:	
	Signer's Signature:	

Service Performed: ☐ Oath ☐ Acknowledgment ☐ Jurat ☐ Other:	**Identification:** ☐ I.D Card ☐ Credible Witness ☐ Drivers License ☐ Known Personally ☐ Passport ☐ Other:	**I.D. Number:**	
		Issued By:	
		Issued Date:	**Expiration Date:**
Document Type:	**Date/Time Notarized:** **AM PM**	**Document Date:**	**Fee Charged:**

Printed Name and Address of Witness:	**Phone Number:**
	Email:
	Witness' Signature:

Comments :	**Record Number:**

NOTARY RECORD

Printed Name and Address of Signer:

Phone Number:

Email:

Signer's Signature:

Thumb Print:

Service Performed:

- ☐ Oath
- ☐ Acknowledgment
- ☐ Jurat
- ☐ Other:

Identification:

- ☐ I.D Card
- ☐ Credible Witness
- ☐ Drivers License
- ☐ Known Personally
- ☐ Passport
- ☐ Other:

I.D. Number:

Issued By:

Issued Date:

Expiration Date:

Document Type:

Date/Time Notarized: AM PM

Document Date:

Fee Charged:

Printed Name and Address of Witness:

Phone Number:

Email:

Witness' Signature:

Comments :

Record Number:

NOTARY RECORD

Printed Name and Address of Signer:

Phone Number:

Email:

Signer's Signature:

Thumb Print:

Service Performed:

- ☐ Oath
- ☐ Acknowledgment
- ☐ Jurat
- ☐ Other:

Identification:

- ☐ I.D Card
- ☐ Credible Witness
- ☐ Drivers License
- ☐ Known Personally
- ☐ Passport
- ☐ Other:

I.D. Number:

Issued By:

Issued Date:

Expiration Date:

Document Type:

Date/Time Notarized: AM PM

Document Date:

Fee Charged:

Printed Name and Address of Witness:

Phone Number:

Email:

Witness' Signature:

Comments :

Record Number:

NOTARY RECORD

Printed Name and Address of Signer:	Phone Number:	Thumb Print:
	Email:	
	Signer's Signature:	

Service Performed:	Identification:		I.D. Number:	
☐ Oath	☐ I.D Card	☐ Credible Witness	Issued By:	
☐ Acknowledgment	☐ Drivers License	☐ Known Personally		
☐ Jurat	☐ Passport		Issued Date:	Expiration Date:
☐ Other:	☐ Other:			
Document Type:	Date/Time Notarized:	AM PM	Document Date:	Fee Charged:

Printed Name and Address of Witness:	Phone Number:
	Email:
	Witness' Signature:

Comments :	Record Number:

NOTARY RECORD

Printed Name and Address of Signer:	Phone Number:	Thumb Print:
	Email:	
	Signer's Signature:	

Service Performed:	Identification:		I.D. Number:	
☐ Oath	☐ I.D Card	☐ Credible Witness	Issued By:	
☐ Acknowledgment	☐ Drivers License	☐ Known Personally		
☐ Jurat	☐ Passport		Issued Date:	Expiration Date:
☐ Other:	☐ Other:			
Document Type:	Date/Time Notarized:	AM PM	Document Date:	Fee Charged:

Printed Name and Address of Witness:	Phone Number:
	Email:
	Witness' Signature:

Comments :	Record Number:

NOTARY RECORD

Printed Name and Address of Signer:	Phone Number:	Thumb Print:
	Email:	
	Signer's Signature:	

Service Performed:	Identification:		I.D. Number:	
☐ Oath	☐ I.D Card	☐ Credible Witness	Issued By:	
☐ Acknowledgment	☐ Drivers License	☐ Known Personally	Issued Date:	Expiration Date:
☐ Jurat	☐ Passport			
☐ Other:	☐ Other:			
Document Type:	Date/Time Notarized: AM PM		Document Date:	Fee Charged:

Printed Name and Address of Witness:	Phone Number:
	Email:
	Witness' Signature:

Comments :	Record Number:

NOTARY RECORD

Printed Name and Address of Signer:	Phone Number:	Thumb Print:
	Email:	
	Signer's Signature:	

Service Performed:	Identification:		I.D. Number:	
☐ Oath	☐ I.D Card	☐ Credible Witness	Issued By:	
☐ Acknowledgment	☐ Drivers License	☐ Known Personally	Issued Date:	Expiration Date:
☐ Jurat	☐ Passport			
☐ Other:	☐ Other:			
Document Type:	Date/Time Notarized: AM PM		Document Date:	Fee Charged:

Printed Name and Address of Witness:	Phone Number:
	Email:
	Witness' Signature:

Comments :	Record Number:

NOTARY RECORD

Printed Name and Address of Signer:	**Phone Number:**	**Thumb Print:**
	Email:	
	Signer's Signature:	

Service Performed: ☐ Oath ☐ Acknowledgment ☐ Jurat ☐ Other:	**Identification:** ☐ I.D Card ☐ Credible Witness ☐ Drivers License ☐ Known Personally ☐ Passport ☐ Other:	**I.D. Number:**	
		Issued By:	
		Issued Date:	**Expiration Date:**
Document Type:	**Date/Time Notarized:** AM PM	**Document Date:**	**Fee Charged:**

Printed Name and Address of Witness:	**Phone Number:**
	Email:
	Witness' Signature:
Comments :	**Record Number:**

NOTARY RECORD

Printed Name and Address of Signer:	**Phone Number:**	**Thumb Print:**
	Email:	
	Signer's Signature:	

Service Performed: ☐ Oath ☐ Acknowledgment ☐ Jurat ☐ Other:	**Identification:** ☐ I.D Card ☐ Credible Witness ☐ Drivers License ☐ Known Personally ☐ Passport ☐ Other:	**I.D. Number:**	
		Issued By:	
		Issued Date:	**Expiration Date:**
Document Type:	**Date/Time Notarized:** AM PM	**Document Date:**	**Fee Charged:**

Printed Name and Address of Witness:	**Phone Number:**
	Email:
	Witness' Signature:
Comments :	**Record Number:**

NOTARY RECORD

Printed Name and Address of Signer:	Phone Number:	Thumb Print:
	Email:	
	Signer's Signature:	

Service Performed:	Identification:		I.D. Number:	
☐ Oath	☐ I.D Card	☐ Credible Witness	Issued By:	
☐ Acknowledgment	☐ Drivers License	☐ Known Personally		
☐ Jurat	☐ Passport		Issued Date:	Expiration Date:
☐ Other:	☐ Other:			
Document Type:	Date/Time Notarized:	AM PM	Document Date:	Fee Charged:

Printed Name and Address of Witness:	Phone Number:
	Email:
	Witness' Signature:

Comments :	Record Number:

NOTARY RECORD

Printed Name and Address of Signer:	Phone Number:	Thumb Print:
	Email:	
	Signer's Signature:	

Service Performed:	Identification:		I.D. Number:	
☐ Oath	☐ I.D Card	☐ Credible Witness	Issued By:	
☐ Acknowledgment	☐ Drivers License	☐ Known Personally		
☐ Jurat	☐ Passport		Issued Date:	Expiration Date:
☐ Other:	☐ Other:			
Document Type:	Date/Time Notarized:	AM PM	Document Date:	Fee Charged:

Printed Name and Address of Witness:	Phone Number:
	Email:
	Witness' Signature:

Comments :	Record Number:

NOTARY RECORD

Printed Name and Address of Signer:	**Phone Number:**	**Thumb Print:**
	Email:	
	Signer's Signature:	

Service Performed: ☐ Oath ☐ Acknowledgment ☐ Jurat ☐ Other:	**Identification:** ☐ I.D Card ☐ Credible Witness ☐ Drivers License ☐ Known Personally ☐ Passport ☐ Other:	**I.D. Number:**	
		Issued By:	
		Issued Date:	**Expiration Date:**
Document Type:	**Date/Time Notarized:** AM PM	**Document Date:**	**Fee Charged:**

Printed Name and Address of Witness:	**Phone Number:**
	Email:
	Witness' Signature:
Comments :	**Record Number:**

NOTARY RECORD

Printed Name and Address of Signer:	**Phone Number:**	**Thumb Print:**
	Email:	
	Signer's Signature:	

Service Performed: ☐ Oath ☐ Acknowledgment ☐ Jurat ☐ Other:	**Identification:** ☐ I.D Card ☐ Credible Witness ☐ Drivers License ☐ Known Personally ☐ Passport ☐ Other:	**I.D. Number:**	
		Issued By:	
		Issued Date:	**Expiration Date:**
Document Type:	**Date/Time Notarized:** AM PM	**Document Date:**	**Fee Charged:**

Printed Name and Address of Witness:	**Phone Number:**
	Email:
	Witness' Signature:
Comments :	**Record Number:**

NOTARY RECORD

Printed Name and Address of Signer:	Phone Number:	Thumb Print:
	Email:	
	Signer's Signature:	

Service Performed:	Identification:		I.D. Number:	
☐ Oath	☐ I.D Card	☐ Credible Witness	Issued By:	
☐ Acknowledgment	☐ Drivers License	☐ Known Personally	Issued Date:	Expiration Date:
☐ Jurat	☐ Passport			
☐ Other:	☐ Other:			
Document Type:	Date/Time Notarized: AM PM		Document Date:	Fee Charged:

Printed Name and Address of Witness:	Phone Number:
	Email:
	Witness' Signature:

Comments :	Record Number:

NOTARY RECORD

Printed Name and Address of Signer:	Phone Number:	Thumb Print:
	Email:	
	Signer's Signature:	

Service Performed:	Identification:		I.D. Number:	
☐ Oath	☐ I.D Card	☐ Credible Witness	Issued By:	
☐ Acknowledgment	☐ Drivers License	☐ Known Personally	Issued Date:	Expiration Date:
☐ Jurat	☐ Passport			
☐ Other:	☐ Other:			
Document Type:	Date/Time Notarized: AM PM		Document Date:	Fee Charged:

Printed Name and Address of Witness:	Phone Number:
	Email:
	Witness' Signature:

Comments :	Record Number:

NOTARY RECORD

Printed Name and Address of Signer:	**Phone Number:**	**Thumb Print:**
	Email:	
	Signer's Signature:	

Service Performed: ☐ Oath ☐ Acknowledgment ☐ Jurat ☐ Other:	**Identification:** ☐ I.D Card ☐ Credible Witness ☐ Drivers License ☐ Known Personally ☐ Passport ☐ Other:	**I.D. Number:**	
		Issued By:	
		Issued Date:	**Expiration Date:**
Document Type:	**Date/Time Notarized:** AM PM	**Document Date:**	**Fee Charged:**

Printed Name and Address of Witness:	**Phone Number:**
	Email:
	Witness' Signature:
Comments :	**Record Number:**

NOTARY RECORD

Printed Name and Address of Signer:	**Phone Number:**	**Thumb Print:**
	Email:	
	Signer's Signature:	

Service Performed: ☐ Oath ☐ Acknowledgment ☐ Jurat ☐ Other:	**Identification:** ☐ I.D Card ☐ Credible Witness ☐ Drivers License ☐ Known Personally ☐ Passport ☐ Other:	**I.D. Number:**	
		Issued By:	
		Issued Date:	**Expiration Date:**
Document Type:	**Date/Time Notarized:** AM PM	**Document Date:**	**Fee Charged:**

Printed Name and Address of Witness:	**Phone Number:**
	Email:
	Witness' Signature:
Comments :	**Record Number:**

NOTARY RECORD

Printed Name and Address of Signer:	**Phone Number:**	**Thumb Print:**
	Email:	
	Signer's Signature:	

Service Performed: ☐ Oath ☐ Acknowledgment ☐ Jurat ☐ Other:	**Identification:** ☐ I.D Card ☐ Credible Witness ☐ Drivers License ☐ Known Personally ☐ Passport ☐ Other:	**I.D. Number:**	
		Issued By:	
		Issued Date:	**Expiration Date:**
Document Type:	**Date/Time Notarized:** AM PM	**Document Date:**	**Fee Charged:**

Printed Name and Address of Witness:	**Phone Number:**
	Email:
	Witness' Signature:
Comments :	**Record Number:**

NOTARY RECORD

Printed Name and Address of Signer:	**Phone Number:**	**Thumb Print:**
	Email:	
	Signer's Signature:	

Service Performed: ☐ Oath ☐ Acknowledgment ☐ Jurat ☐ Other:	**Identification:** ☐ I.D Card ☐ Credible Witness ☐ Drivers License ☐ Known Personally ☐ Passport ☐ Other:	**I.D. Number:**	
		Issued By:	
		Issued Date:	**Expiration Date:**
Document Type:	**Date/Time Notarized:** AM PM	**Document Date:**	**Fee Charged:**

Printed Name and Address of Witness:	**Phone Number:**
	Email:
	Witness' Signature:
Comments :	**Record Number:**

NOTARY RECORD

Printed Name and Address of Signer:	**Phone Number:**	**Thumb Print:**
	Email:	
	Signer's Signature:	

Service Performed: ☐ Oath ☐ Acknowledgment ☐ Jurat ☐ Other:	**Identification:** ☐ I.D Card ☐ Credible Witness ☐ Drivers License ☐ Known Personally ☐ Passport ☐ Other:	**I.D. Number:**	
		Issued By:	
		Issued Date:	**Expiration Date:**
Document Type:	**Date/Time Notarized:** **AM** **PM**	**Document Date:**	**Fee Charged:**

Printed Name and Address of Witness:	**Phone Number:**
	Email:
	Witness' Signature:

Comments :	**Record Number:**

NOTARY RECORD

Printed Name and Address of Signer:	**Phone Number:**	**Thumb Print:**
	Email:	
	Signer's Signature:	

Service Performed: ☐ Oath ☐ Acknowledgment ☐ Jurat ☐ Other:	**Identification:** ☐ I.D Card ☐ Credible Witness ☐ Drivers License ☐ Known Personally ☐ Passport ☐ Other:	**I.D. Number:**	
		Issued By:	
		Issued Date:	**Expiration Date:**
Document Type:	**Date/Time Notarized:** **AM** **PM**	**Document Date:**	**Fee Charged:**

Printed Name and Address of Witness:	**Phone Number:**
	Email:
	Witness' Signature:

Comments :	**Record Number:**

NOTARY RECORD

Printed Name and Address of Signer:

Phone Number:

Email:

Signer's Signature:

Thumb Print:

Service Performed:
- ☐ Oath
- ☐ Acknowledgment
- ☐ Jurat
- ☐ Other:

Identification:
- ☐ I.D Card
- ☐ Credible Witness
- ☐ Drivers License
- ☐ Known Personally
- ☐ Passport
- ☐ Other:

I.D. Number:

Issued By:

Issued Date:

Expiration Date:

Document Type:

Date/Time Notarized: **AM** **PM**

Document Date:

Fee Charged:

Printed Name and Address of Witness:

Phone Number:

Email:

Witness' Signature:

Comments :

Record Number:

NOTARY RECORD

Printed Name and Address of Signer:

Phone Number:

Email:

Signer's Signature:

Thumb Print:

Service Performed:
- ☐ Oath
- ☐ Acknowledgment
- ☐ Jurat
- ☐ Other:

Identification:
- ☐ I.D Card
- ☐ Credible Witness
- ☐ Drivers License
- ☐ Known Personally
- ☐ Passport
- ☐ Other:

I.D. Number:

Issued By:

Issued Date:

Expiration Date:

Document Type:

Date/Time Notarized: **AM** **PM**

Document Date:

Fee Charged:

Printed Name and Address of Witness:

Phone Number:

Email:

Witness' Signature:

Comments :

Record Number:

NOTARY RECORD

Printed Name and Address of Signer:	**Phone Number:**	**Thumb Print:**
	Email:	
	Signer's Signature:	

Service Performed: ☐ Oath ☐ Acknowledgment ☐ Jurat ☐ Other:	**Identification:** ☐ I.D Card ☐ Credible Witness ☐ Drivers License ☐ Known Personally ☐ Passport ☐ Other:	**I.D. Number:**	
		Issued By:	
		Issued Date:	**Expiration Date:**
Document Type:	**Date/Time Notarized:** AM PM	**Document Date:**	**Fee Charged:**

Printed Name and Address of Witness:	**Phone Number:**
	Email:
	Witness' Signature:

Comments :	**Record Number:**

NOTARY RECORD

Printed Name and Address of Signer:	**Phone Number:**	**Thumb Print:**
	Email:	
	Signer's Signature:	

Service Performed: ☐ Oath ☐ Acknowledgment ☐ Jurat ☐ Other:	**Identification:** ☐ I.D Card ☐ Credible Witness ☐ Drivers License ☐ Known Personally ☐ Passport ☐ Other:	**I.D. Number:**	
		Issued By:	
		Issued Date:	**Expiration Date:**
Document Type:	**Date/Time Notarized:** AM PM	**Document Date:**	**Fee Charged:**

Printed Name and Address of Witness:	**Phone Number:**
	Email:
	Witness' Signature:

Comments :	**Record Number:**

NOTARY RECORD

Printed Name and Address of Signer:	Phone Number:	Thumb Print:
	Email:	
	Signer's Signature:	

Service Performed:	Identification:		I.D. Number:	
☐ Oath	☐ I.D Card	☐ Credible Witness	Issued By:	
☐ Acknowledgment	☐ Drivers License	☐ Known Personally		
☐ Jurat	☐ Passport		Issued Date:	Expiration Date:
☐ Other:	☐ Other:			
Document Type:	Date/Time Notarized: AM PM		Document Date:	Fee Charged:

Printed Name and Address of Witness:	Phone Number:
	Email:
	Witness' Signature:

Comments :	Record Number:

NOTARY RECORD

Printed Name and Address of Signer:	Phone Number:	Thumb Print:
	Email:	
	Signer's Signature:	

Service Performed:	Identification:		I.D. Number:	
☐ Oath	☐ I.D Card	☐ Credible Witness	Issued By:	
☐ Acknowledgment	☐ Drivers License	☐ Known Personally		
☐ Jurat	☐ Passport		Issued Date:	Expiration Date:
☐ Other:	☐ Other:			
Document Type:	Date/Time Notarized: AM PM		Document Date:	Fee Charged:

Printed Name and Address of Witness:	Phone Number:
	Email:
	Witness' Signature:

Comments :	Record Number:

NOTARY RECORD

Printed Name and Address of Signer:	Phone Number:	Thumb Print:
	Email:	
	Signer's Signature:	

Service Performed:	Identification:		I.D. Number:	
☐ Oath	☐ I.D Card	☐ Credible Witness	Issued By:	
☐ Acknowledgment	☐ Drivers License	☐ Known Personally	Issued Date:	Expiration Date:
☐ Jurat	☐ Passport			
☐ Other:	☐ Other:			
Document Type:	Date/Time Notarized: AM PM		Document Date:	Fee Charged:

Printed Name and Address of Witness:	Phone Number:
	Email:
	Witness' Signature:

Comments :	Record Number:

NOTARY RECORD

Printed Name and Address of Signer:	Phone Number:	Thumb Print:
	Email:	
	Signer's Signature:	

Service Performed:	Identification:		I.D. Number:	
☐ Oath	☐ I.D Card	☐ Credible Witness	Issued By:	
☐ Acknowledgment	☐ Drivers License	☐ Known Personally	Issued Date:	Expiration Date:
☐ Jurat	☐ Passport			
☐ Other:	☐ Other:			
Document Type:	Date/Time Notarized: AM PM		Document Date:	Fee Charged:

Printed Name and Address of Witness:	Phone Number:
	Email:
	Witness' Signature:

Comments :	Record Number:

NOTARY RECORD

Printed Name and Address of Signer:	**Phone Number:**	**Thumb Print:**
	Email:	
	Signer's Signature:	

Service Performed: ☐ Oath ☐ Acknowledgment ☐ Jurat ☐ Other:	**Identification:** ☐ I.D Card ☐ Credible Witness ☐ Drivers License ☐ Known Personally ☐ Passport ☐ Other:	**I.D. Number:**	
		Issued By:	
		Issued Date:	**Expiration Date:**
Document Type:	**Date/Time Notarized:** AM PM	**Document Date:**	**Fee Charged:**

Printed Name and Address of Witness:	**Phone Number:**
	Email:
	Witness' Signature:
Comments :	**Record Number:**

NOTARY RECORD

Printed Name and Address of Signer:	**Phone Number:**	**Thumb Print:**
	Email:	
	Signer's Signature:	

Service Performed: ☐ Oath ☐ Acknowledgment ☐ Jurat ☐ Other:	**Identification:** ☐ I.D Card ☐ Credible Witness ☐ Drivers License ☐ Known Personally ☐ Passport ☐ Other:	**I.D. Number:**	
		Issued By:	
		Issued Date:	**Expiration Date:**
Document Type:	**Date/Time Notarized:** AM PM	**Document Date:**	**Fee Charged:**

Printed Name and Address of Witness:	**Phone Number:**
	Email:
	Witness' Signature:
Comments :	**Record Number:**

NOTARY RECORD

Printed Name and Address of Signer:	Phone Number:	Thumb Print:
	Email:	
	Signer's Signature:	

Service Performed:	Identification:		I.D. Number:	
☐ Oath	☐ I.D Card	☐ Credible Witness	Issued By:	
☐ Acknowledgment	☐ Drivers License	☐ Known Personally	Issued Date:	Expiration Date:
☐ Jurat	☐ Passport			
☐ Other:	☐ Other:			

Document Type:	Date/Time Notarized: AM PM	Document Date:	Fee Charged:

Printed Name and Address of Witness:	Phone Number:
	Email:
	Witness' Signature:

Comments :	Record Number:

NOTARY RECORD

Printed Name and Address of Signer:	Phone Number:	Thumb Print:
	Email:	
	Signer's Signature:	

Service Performed:	Identification:		I.D. Number:	
☐ Oath	☐ I.D Card	☐ Credible Witness	Issued By:	
☐ Acknowledgment	☐ Drivers License	☐ Known Personally	Issued Date:	Expiration Date:
☐ Jurat	☐ Passport			
☐ Other:	☐ Other:			

Document Type:	Date/Time Notarized: AM PM	Document Date:	Fee Charged:

Printed Name and Address of Witness:	Phone Number:
	Email:
	Witness' Signature:

Comments :	Record Number:

NOTARY RECORD

Printed Name and Address of Signer:	**Phone Number:**	**Thumb Print:**
	Email:	
	Signer's Signature:	

Service Performed: ☐ Oath ☐ Acknowledgment ☐ Jurat ☐ Other:	**Identification:** ☐ I.D Card ☐ Credible Witness ☐ Drivers License ☐ Known Personally ☐ Passport ☐ Other:	**I.D. Number:**	
		Issued By:	
		Issued Date:	**Expiration Date:**
Document Type:	**Date/Time Notarized:** **AM** **PM**	**Document Date:**	**Fee Charged:**

Printed Name and Address of Witness:	**Phone Number:**
	Email:
	Witness' Signature:

Comments :	**Record Number:**

NOTARY RECORD

Printed Name and Address of Signer:	**Phone Number:**	**Thumb Print:**
	Email:	
	Signer's Signature:	

Service Performed: ☐ Oath ☐ Acknowledgment ☐ Jurat ☐ Other:	**Identification:** ☐ I.D Card ☐ Credible Witness ☐ Drivers License ☐ Known Personally ☐ Passport ☐ Other:	**I.D. Number:**	
		Issued By:	
		Issued Date:	**Expiration Date:**
Document Type:	**Date/Time Notarized:** **AM** **PM**	**Document Date:**	**Fee Charged:**

Printed Name and Address of Witness:	**Phone Number:**
	Email:
	Witness' Signature:

Comments :	**Record Number:**

NOTARY RECORD

Printed Name and Address of Signer:	**Phone Number:**	**Thumb Print:**
	Email:	
	Signer's Signature:	

Service Performed: ☐ Oath ☐ Acknowledgment ☐ Jurat ☐ Other:	**Identification:** ☐ I.D Card ☐ Credible Witness ☐ Drivers License ☐ Known Personally ☐ Passport ☐ Other:	**I.D. Number:**	
		Issued By:	
		Issued Date:	**Expiration Date:**
Document Type:	**Date/Time Notarized:** AM PM	**Document Date:**	**Fee Charged:**

Printed Name and Address of Witness:	**Phone Number:**
	Email:
	Witness' Signature:
Comments :	**Record Number:**

NOTARY RECORD

Printed Name and Address of Signer:	**Phone Number:**	**Thumb Print:**
	Email:	
	Signer's Signature:	

Service Performed: ☐ Oath ☐ Acknowledgment ☐ Jurat ☐ Other:	**Identification:** ☐ I.D Card ☐ Credible Witness ☐ Drivers License ☐ Known Personally ☐ Passport ☐ Other:	**I.D. Number:**	
		Issued By:	
		Issued Date:	**Expiration Date:**
Document Type:	**Date/Time Notarized:** AM PM	**Document Date:**	**Fee Charged:**

Printed Name and Address of Witness:	**Phone Number:**
	Email:
	Witness' Signature:
Comments :	**Record Number:**

NOTARY RECORD

Printed Name and Address of Signer:	Phone Number:	Thumb Print:
	Email:	
	Signer's Signature:	

Service Performed:	Identification:		I.D. Number:	
☐ Oath	☐ I.D Card	☐ Credible Witness	Issued By:	
☐ Acknowledgment	☐ Drivers License	☐ Known Personally	Issued Date:	Expiration Date:
☐ Jurat	☐ Passport			
☐ Other:	☐ Other:			
Document Type:	Date/Time Notarized: AM PM		Document Date:	Fee Charged:

Printed Name and Address of Witness:	Phone Number:
	Email:
	Witness' Signature:

Comments :	Record Number:

NOTARY RECORD

Printed Name and Address of Signer:	Phone Number:	Thumb Print:
	Email:	
	Signer's Signature:	

Service Performed:	Identification:		I.D. Number:	
☐ Oath	☐ I.D Card	☐ Credible Witness	Issued By:	
☐ Acknowledgment	☐ Drivers License	☐ Known Personally	Issued Date:	Expiration Date:
☐ Jurat	☐ Passport			
☐ Other:	☐ Other:			
Document Type:	Date/Time Notarized: AM PM		Document Date:	Fee Charged:

Printed Name and Address of Witness:	Phone Number:
	Email:
	Witness' Signature:

Comments :	Record Number:

NOTARY RECORD

Printed Name and Address of Signer:	**Phone Number:**	**Thumb Print:**
	Email:	
	Signer's Signature:	

Service Performed: ☐ Oath ☐ Acknowledgment ☐ Jurat ☐ Other:	**Identification:** ☐ I.D Card ☐ Credible Witness ☐ Drivers License ☐ Known Personally ☐ Passport ☐ Other:	**I.D. Number:**	
		Issued By:	
		Issued Date:	**Expiration Date:**
Document Type:	**Date/Time Notarized:** AM PM	**Document Date:**	**Fee Charged:**

Printed Name and Address of Witness:	**Phone Number:**
	Email:
	Witness' Signature:
Comments :	**Record Number:**

NOTARY RECORD

Printed Name and Address of Signer:	**Phone Number:**	**Thumb Print:**
	Email:	
	Signer's Signature:	

Service Performed: ☐ Oath ☐ Acknowledgment ☐ Jurat ☐ Other:	**Identification:** ☐ I.D Card ☐ Credible Witness ☐ Drivers License ☐ Known Personally ☐ Passport ☐ Other:	**I.D. Number:**	
		Issued By:	
		Issued Date:	**Expiration Date:**
Document Type:	**Date/Time Notarized:** AM PM	**Document Date:**	**Fee Charged:**

Printed Name and Address of Witness:	**Phone Number:**
	Email:
	Witness' Signature:
Comments :	**Record Number:**

NOTARY RECORD

Printed Name and Address of Signer:	**Phone Number:**	**Thumb Print:**
	Email:	
	Signer's Signature:	

Service Performed: ☐ Oath ☐ Acknowledgment ☐ Jurat ☐ Other:	**Identification:** ☐ I.D Card ☐ Credible Witness ☐ Drivers License ☐ Known Personally ☐ Passport ☐ Other:	**I.D. Number:**	
		Issued By:	
		Issued Date:	**Expiration Date:**
Document Type:	**Date/Time Notarized:** AM PM	**Document Date:**	**Fee Charged:**

Printed Name and Address of Witness:	**Phone Number:**
	Email:
	Witness' Signature:

Comments :	**Record Number:**

NOTARY RECORD

Printed Name and Address of Signer:	**Phone Number:**	**Thumb Print:**
	Email:	
	Signer's Signature:	

Service Performed: ☐ Oath ☐ Acknowledgment ☐ Jurat ☐ Other:	**Identification:** ☐ I.D Card ☐ Credible Witness ☐ Drivers License ☐ Known Personally ☐ Passport ☐ Other:	**I.D. Number:**	
		Issued By:	
		Issued Date:	**Expiration Date:**
Document Type:	**Date/Time Notarized:** AM PM	**Document Date:**	**Fee Charged:**

Printed Name and Address of Witness:	**Phone Number:**
	Email:
	Witness' Signature:

Comments :	**Record Number:**

NOTARY RECORD

Printed Name and Address of Signer:	Phone Number:	Thumb Print:
	Email:	
	Signer's Signature:	

Service Performed:	Identification:		I.D. Number:	
☐ Oath	☐ I.D Card	☐ Credible Witness	Issued By:	
☐ Acknowledgment	☐ Drivers License	☐ Known Personally	Issued Date:	Expiration Date:
☐ Jurat	☐ Passport			
☐ Other:	☐ Other:			
Document Type:	Date/Time Notarized: AM PM		Document Date:	Fee Charged:

Printed Name and Address of Witness:	Phone Number:
	Email:
	Witness' Signature:

Comments :	Record Number:

NOTARY RECORD

Printed Name and Address of Signer:	Phone Number:	Thumb Print:
	Email:	
	Signer's Signature:	

Service Performed:	Identification:		I.D. Number:	
☐ Oath	☐ I.D Card	☐ Credible Witness	Issued By:	
☐ Acknowledgment	☐ Drivers License	☐ Known Personally	Issued Date:	Expiration Date:
☐ Jurat	☐ Passport			
☐ Other:	☐ Other:			
Document Type:	Date/Time Notarized: AM PM		Document Date:	Fee Charged:

Printed Name and Address of Witness:	Phone Number:
	Email:
	Witness' Signature:

Comments :	Record Number:

NOTARY RECORD

Printed Name and Address of Signer:	Phone Number:	Thumb Print:
	Email:	
	Signer's Signature:	

Service Performed:	Identification:		I.D. Number:	
☐ Oath	☐ I.D Card	☐ Credible Witness		
☐ Acknowledgment	☐ Drivers License	☐ Known Personally	Issued By:	
☐ Jurat	☐ Passport			
☐ Other:	☐ Other:		Issued Date:	Expiration Date:
Document Type:	Date/Time Notarized: AM PM		Document Date:	Fee Charged:

Printed Name and Address of Witness:	Phone Number:
	Email:
	Witness' Signature:

Comments :	Record Number:

NOTARY RECORD

Printed Name and Address of Signer:	Phone Number:	Thumb Print:
	Email:	
	Signer's Signature:	

Service Performed:	Identification:		I.D. Number:	
☐ Oath	☐ I.D Card	☐ Credible Witness		
☐ Acknowledgment	☐ Drivers License	☐ Known Personally	Issued By:	
☐ Jurat	☐ Passport			
☐ Other:	☐ Other:		Issued Date:	Expiration Date:
Document Type:	Date/Time Notarized: AM PM		Document Date:	Fee Charged:

Printed Name and Address of Witness:	Phone Number:
	Email:
	Witness' Signature:

Comments :	Record Number:

NOTARY RECORD

Printed Name and Address of Signer:	Phone Number:	Thumb Print:
	Email:	
	Signer's Signature:	

Service Performed:	Identification:		I.D. Number:	
☐ Oath	☐ I.D Card	☐ Credible Witness		
☐ Acknowledgment	☐ Drivers License	☐ Known Personally	Issued By:	
☐ Jurat	☐ Passport			
☐ Other:	☐ Other:		Issued Date:	Expiration Date:
Document Type:	Date/Time Notarized:	AM PM	Document Date:	Fee Charged:

Printed Name and Address of Witness:	Phone Number:
	Email:
	Witness' Signature:

Comments :	Record Number:

NOTARY RECORD

Printed Name and Address of Signer:	Phone Number:	Thumb Print:
	Email:	
	Signer's Signature:	

Service Performed:	Identification:		I.D. Number:	
☐ Oath	☐ I.D Card	☐ Credible Witness		
☐ Acknowledgment	☐ Drivers License	☐ Known Personally	Issued By:	
☐ Jurat	☐ Passport			
☐ Other:	☐ Other:		Issued Date:	Expiration Date:
Document Type:	Date/Time Notarized:	AM PM	Document Date:	Fee Charged:

Printed Name and Address of Witness:	Phone Number:
	Email:
	Witness' Signature:

Comments :	Record Number:

NOTARY RECORD

Printed Name and Address of Signer:	Phone Number:	Thumb Print:
	Email:	
	Signer's Signature:	

Service Performed:	Identification:		I.D. Number:	
☐ Oath	☐ I.D Card	☐ Credible Witness		
☐ Acknowledgment	☐ Drivers License	☐ Known Personally	Issued By:	
☐ Jurat	☐ Passport			
☐ Other:	☐ Other:		Issued Date:	Expiration Date:
Document Type:	Date/Time Notarized:	AM PM	Document Date:	Fee Charged:

Printed Name and Address of Witness:	Phone Number:
	Email:
	Witness' Signature:

Comments :	Record Number:

NOTARY RECORD

Printed Name and Address of Signer:	Phone Number:	Thumb Print:
	Email:	
	Signer's Signature:	

Service Performed:	Identification:		I.D. Number:	
☐ Oath	☐ I.D Card	☐ Credible Witness		
☐ Acknowledgment	☐ Drivers License	☐ Known Personally	Issued By:	
☐ Jurat	☐ Passport			
☐ Other:	☐ Other:		Issued Date:	Expiration Date:
Document Type:	Date/Time Notarized:	AM PM	Document Date:	Fee Charged:

Printed Name and Address of Witness:	Phone Number:
	Email:
	Witness' Signature:

Comments :	Record Number:

NOTARY RECORD

Printed Name and Address of Signer:	**Phone Number:**	**Thumb Print:**
	Email:	
	Signer's Signature:	

Service Performed: ☐ Oath ☐ Acknowledgment ☐ Jurat ☐ Other:	**Identification:** ☐ I.D Card ☐ Credible Witness ☐ Drivers License ☐ Known Personally ☐ Passport ☐ Other:	**I.D. Number:**	
		Issued By:	
		Issued Date:	**Expiration Date:**
Document Type:	**Date/Time Notarized:** AM PM	**Document Date:**	**Fee Charged:**

Printed Name and Address of Witness:	**Phone Number:**
	Email:
	Witness' Signature:
Comments :	**Record Number:**

NOTARY RECORD

Printed Name and Address of Signer:	**Phone Number:**	**Thumb Print:**
	Email:	
	Signer's Signature:	

Service Performed: ☐ Oath ☐ Acknowledgment ☐ Jurat ☐ Other:	**Identification:** ☐ I.D Card ☐ Credible Witness ☐ Drivers License ☐ Known Personally ☐ Passport ☐ Other:	**I.D. Number:**	
		Issued By:	
		Issued Date:	**Expiration Date:**
Document Type:	**Date/Time Notarized:** AM PM	**Document Date:**	**Fee Charged:**

Printed Name and Address of Witness:	**Phone Number:**
	Email:
	Witness' Signature:
Comments :	**Record Number:**

NOTARY RECORD

Printed Name and Address of Signer:	Phone Number:	Thumb Print:
	Email:	
	Signer's Signature:	

Service Performed:	Identification:		I.D. Number:	
☐ Oath	☐ I.D Card	☐ Credible Witness	Issued By:	
☐ Acknowledgment	☐ Drivers License	☐ Known Personally	Issued Date:	Expiration Date:
☐ Jurat	☐ Passport			
☐ Other:	☐ Other:			
Document Type:	Date/Time Notarized: AM PM		Document Date:	Fee Charged:

Printed Name and Address of Witness:	Phone Number:
	Email:
	Witness' Signature:

Comments :	Record Number:

NOTARY RECORD

Printed Name and Address of Signer:	Phone Number:	Thumb Print:
	Email:	
	Signer's Signature:	

Service Performed:	Identification:		I.D. Number:	
☐ Oath	☐ I.D Card	☐ Credible Witness	Issued By:	
☐ Acknowledgment	☐ Drivers License	☐ Known Personally	Issued Date:	Expiration Date:
☐ Jurat	☐ Passport			
☐ Other:	☐ Other:			
Document Type:	Date/Time Notarized: AM PM		Document Date:	Fee Charged:

Printed Name and Address of Witness:	Phone Number:
	Email:
	Witness' Signature:

Comments :	Record Number:

NOTARY RECORD

Printed Name and Address of Signer:

Phone Number:

Email:

Signer's Signature:

Thumb Print:

Service Performed:
- ☐ Oath
- ☐ Acknowledgment
- ☐ Jurat
- ☐ Other:

Identification:
- ☐ I.D Card
- ☐ Credible Witness
- ☐ Drivers License
- ☐ Known Personally
- ☐ Passport
- ☐ Other:

I.D. Number:

Issued By:

Issued Date:

Expiration Date:

Document Type:

Date/Time Notarized: **AM** **PM**

Document Date:

Fee Charged:

Printed Name and Address of Witness:

Phone Number:

Email:

Witness' Signature:

Comments :

Record Number:

NOTARY RECORD

Printed Name and Address of Signer:

Phone Number:

Email:

Signer's Signature:

Thumb Print:

Service Performed:
- ☐ Oath
- ☐ Acknowledgment
- ☐ Jurat
- ☐ Other:

Identification:
- ☐ I.D Card
- ☐ Credible Witness
- ☐ Drivers License
- ☐ Known Personally
- ☐ Passport
- ☐ Other:

I.D. Number:

Issued By:

Issued Date:

Expiration Date:

Document Type:

Date/Time Notarized: **AM** **PM**

Document Date:

Fee Charged:

Printed Name and Address of Witness:

Phone Number:

Email:

Witness' Signature:

Comments :

Record Number:

NOTARY RECORD

Printed Name and Address of Signer:	**Phone Number:**	**Thumb Print:**
	Email:	
	Signer's Signature:	

Service Performed: ☐ Oath ☐ Acknowledgment ☐ Jurat ☐ Other:	**Identification:** ☐ I.D Card ☐ Credible Witness ☐ Drivers License ☐ Known Personally ☐ Passport ☐ Other:	**I.D. Number:**	
		Issued By:	
		Issued Date:	**Expiration Date:**
Document Type:	**Date/Time Notarized:** AM PM	**Document Date:**	**Fee Charged:**

Printed Name and Address of Witness:	**Phone Number:**
	Email:
	Witness' Signature:
Comments :	**Record Number:**

NOTARY RECORD

Printed Name and Address of Signer:	**Phone Number:**	**Thumb Print:**
	Email:	
	Signer's Signature:	

Service Performed: ☐ Oath ☐ Acknowledgment ☐ Jurat ☐ Other:	**Identification:** ☐ I.D Card ☐ Credible Witness ☐ Drivers License ☐ Known Personally ☐ Passport ☐ Other:	**I.D. Number:**	
		Issued By:	
		Issued Date:	**Expiration Date:**
Document Type:	**Date/Time Notarized:** AM PM	**Document Date:**	**Fee Charged:**

Printed Name and Address of Witness:	**Phone Number:**
	Email:
	Witness' Signature:
Comments :	**Record Number:**

NOTARY RECORD

Printed Name and Address of Signer:

Phone Number:

Email:

Signer's Signature:

Thumb Print:

Service Performed:

- ☐ Oath
- ☐ Acknowledgment
- ☐ Jurat
- ☐ Other:

Identification:

- ☐ I.D Card
- ☐ Credible Witness
- ☐ Drivers License
- ☐ Known Personally
- ☐ Passport
- ☐ Other:

I.D. Number:

Issued By:

Issued Date:

Expiration Date:

Document Type:

Date/Time Notarized: **AM** **PM**

Document Date:

Fee Charged:

Printed Name and Address of Witness:

Phone Number:

Email:

Witness' Signature:

Comments :

Record Number:

NOTARY RECORD

Printed Name and Address of Signer:

Phone Number:

Email:

Signer's Signature:

Thumb Print:

Service Performed:

- ☐ Oath
- ☐ Acknowledgment
- ☐ Jurat
- ☐ Other:

Identification:

- ☐ I.D Card
- ☐ Credible Witness
- ☐ Drivers License
- ☐ Known Personally
- ☐ Passport
- ☐ Other:

I.D. Number:

Issued By:

Issued Date:

Expiration Date:

Document Type:

Date/Time Notarized: **AM** **PM**

Document Date:

Fee Charged:

Printed Name and Address of Witness:

Phone Number:

Email:

Witness' Signature:

Comments :

Record Number:

NOTARY RECORD

Printed Name and Address of Signer:	Phone Number:	Thumb Print:
	Email:	
	Signer's Signature:	

Service Performed:	Identification:		I.D. Number:	
☐ Oath	☐ I.D Card	☐ Credible Witness		
☐ Acknowledgment	☐ Drivers License	☐ Known Personally	Issued By:	
☐ Jurat	☐ Passport			
☐ Other:	☐ Other:		Issued Date:	Expiration Date:
Document Type:	Date/Time Notarized:	AM PM	Document Date:	Fee Charged:

Printed Name and Address of Witness:	Phone Number:
	Email:
	Witness' Signature:

Comments :	Record Number:

NOTARY RECORD

Printed Name and Address of Signer:	Phone Number:	Thumb Print:
	Email:	
	Signer's Signature:	

Service Performed:	Identification:		I.D. Number:	
☐ Oath	☐ I.D Card	☐ Credible Witness		
☐ Acknowledgment	☐ Drivers License	☐ Known Personally	Issued By:	
☐ Jurat	☐ Passport			
☐ Other:	☐ Other:		Issued Date:	Expiration Date:
Document Type:	Date/Time Notarized:	AM PM	Document Date:	Fee Charged:

Printed Name and Address of Witness:	Phone Number:
	Email:
	Witness' Signature:

Comments :	Record Number:

NOTARY RECORD

Printed Name and Address of Signer:	**Phone Number:**	**Thumb Print:**
	Email:	
	Signer's Signature:	

Service Performed: ☐ Oath ☐ Acknowledgment ☐ Jurat ☐ Other:	**Identification:** ☐ I.D Card ☐ Credible Witness ☐ Drivers License ☐ Known Personally ☐ Passport ☐ Other:	**I.D. Number:**	
		Issued By:	
		Issued Date:	**Expiration Date:**
Document Type:	**Date/Time Notarized:** AM PM	**Document Date:**	**Fee Charged:**

Printed Name and Address of Witness:	**Phone Number:**
	Email:
	Witness' Signature:
Comments :	**Record Number:**

NOTARY RECORD

Printed Name and Address of Signer:	**Phone Number:**	**Thumb Print:**
	Email:	
	Signer's Signature:	

Service Performed: ☐ Oath ☐ Acknowledgment ☐ Jurat ☐ Other:	**Identification:** ☐ I.D Card ☐ Credible Witness ☐ Drivers License ☐ Known Personally ☐ Passport ☐ Other:	**I.D. Number:**	
		Issued By:	
		Issued Date:	**Expiration Date:**
Document Type:	**Date/Time Notarized:** AM PM	**Document Date:**	**Fee Charged:**

Printed Name and Address of Witness:	**Phone Number:**
	Email:
	Witness' Signature:
Comments :	**Record Number:**

NOTARY RECORD

Printed Name and Address of Signer:	Phone Number:	Thumb Print:
	Email:	
	Signer's Signature:	

Service Performed:	Identification:		I.D. Number:	
☐ Oath	☐ I.D Card	☐ Credible Witness		
☐ Acknowledgment	☐ Drivers License	☐ Known Personally	Issued By:	
☐ Jurat	☐ Passport			
☐ Other:	☐ Other:		Issued Date:	Expiration Date:
Document Type:	Date/Time Notarized: AM PM		Document Date:	Fee Charged:

Printed Name and Address of Witness:	Phone Number:
	Email:
	Witness' Signature:

Comments :	Record Number:

NOTARY RECORD

Printed Name and Address of Signer:	Phone Number:	Thumb Print:
	Email:	
	Signer's Signature:	

Service Performed:	Identification:		I.D. Number:	
☐ Oath	☐ I.D Card	☐ Credible Witness		
☐ Acknowledgment	☐ Drivers License	☐ Known Personally	Issued By:	
☐ Jurat	☐ Passport			
☐ Other:	☐ Other:		Issued Date:	Expiration Date:
Document Type:	Date/Time Notarized: AM PM		Document Date:	Fee Charged:

Printed Name and Address of Witness:	Phone Number:
	Email:
	Witness' Signature:

Comments :	Record Number:

NOTARY RECORD

Printed Name and Address of Signer:	**Phone Number:**	**Thumb Print:**
	Email:	
	Signer's Signature:	

Service Performed: ☐ Oath ☐ Acknowledgment ☐ Jurat ☐ Other:	**Identification:** ☐ I.D Card ☐ Credible Witness ☐ Drivers License ☐ Known Personally ☐ Passport ☐ Other:	**I.D. Number:**	
		Issued By:	
		Issued Date:	**Expiration Date:**
Document Type:	**Date/Time Notarized:** AM PM	**Document Date:**	**Fee Charged:**

Printed Name and Address of Witness:	**Phone Number:**
	Email:
	Witness' Signature:
Comments :	**Record Number:**

NOTARY RECORD

Printed Name and Address of Signer:	**Phone Number:**	**Thumb Print:**
	Email:	
	Signer's Signature:	

Service Performed: ☐ Oath ☐ Acknowledgment ☐ Jurat ☐ Other:	**Identification:** ☐ I.D Card ☐ Credible Witness ☐ Drivers License ☐ Known Personally ☐ Passport ☐ Other:	**I.D. Number:**	
		Issued By:	
		Issued Date:	**Expiration Date:**
Document Type:	**Date/Time Notarized:** AM PM	**Document Date:**	**Fee Charged:**

Printed Name and Address of Witness:	**Phone Number:**
	Email:
	Witness' Signature:
Comments :	**Record Number:**

NOTARY RECORD

Printed Name and Address of Signer:	Phone Number:	Thumb Print:
	Email:	
	Signer's Signature:	

Service Performed:
- ☐ Oath
- ☐ Acknowledgment
- ☐ Jurat
- ☐ Other:

Identification:
- ☐ I.D Card
- ☐ Credible Witness
- ☐ Drivers License
- ☐ Known Personally
- ☐ Passport
- ☐ Other:

I.D. Number:	
Issued By:	
Issued Date:	Expiration Date:

Document Type:	Date/Time Notarized: AM PM	Document Date:	Fee Charged:

Printed Name and Address of Witness:	Phone Number:
	Email:
	Witness' Signature:

Comments :	Record Number:

NOTARY RECORD

Printed Name and Address of Signer:	Phone Number:	Thumb Print:
	Email:	
	Signer's Signature:	

Service Performed:
- ☐ Oath
- ☐ Acknowledgment
- ☐ Jurat
- ☐ Other:

Identification:
- ☐ I.D Card
- ☐ Credible Witness
- ☐ Drivers License
- ☐ Known Personally
- ☐ Passport
- ☐ Other:

I.D. Number:	
Issued By:	
Issued Date:	Expiration Date:

Document Type:	Date/Time Notarized: AM PM	Document Date:	Fee Charged:

Printed Name and Address of Witness:	Phone Number:
	Email:
	Witness' Signature:

Comments :	Record Number:

NOTARY RECORD

Printed Name and Address of Signer:	Phone Number:	Thumb Print:
	Email:	
	Signer's Signature:	

Service Performed:	Identification:		I.D. Number:	
☐ Oath	☐ I.D Card	☐ Credible Witness		
☐ Acknowledgment	☐ Drivers License	☐ Known Personally	Issued By:	
☐ Jurat	☐ Passport			
☐ Other:	☐ Other:		Issued Date:	Expiration Date:
Document Type:	Date/Time Notarized: AM PM		Document Date:	Fee Charged:

Printed Name and Address of Witness:	Phone Number:
	Email:
	Witness' Signature:

Comments :	Record Number:

NOTARY RECORD

Printed Name and Address of Signer:	Phone Number:	Thumb Print:
	Email:	
	Signer's Signature:	

Service Performed:	Identification:		I.D. Number:	
☐ Oath	☐ I.D Card	☐ Credible Witness		
☐ Acknowledgment	☐ Drivers License	☐ Known Personally	Issued By:	
☐ Jurat	☐ Passport			
☐ Other:	☐ Other:		Issued Date:	Expiration Date:
Document Type:	Date/Time Notarized: AM PM		Document Date:	Fee Charged:

Printed Name and Address of Witness:	Phone Number:
	Email:
	Witness' Signature:

Comments :	Record Number:

NOTARY RECORD

Printed Name and Address of Signer:	**Phone Number:**	**Thumb Print:**
	Email:	
	Signer's Signature:	

Service Performed: ☐ Oath ☐ Acknowledgment ☐ Jurat ☐ Other:	**Identification:** ☐ I.D Card ☐ Credible Witness ☐ Drivers License ☐ Known Personally ☐ Passport ☐ Other:	**I.D. Number:**	
		Issued By:	
		Issued Date:	**Expiration Date:**
Document Type:	**Date/Time Notarized:** AM PM	**Document Date:**	**Fee Charged:**

Printed Name and Address of Witness:	**Phone Number:**
	Email:
	Witness' Signature:
Comments :	**Record Number:**

NOTARY RECORD

Printed Name and Address of Signer:	**Phone Number:**	**Thumb Print:**
	Email:	
	Signer's Signature:	

Service Performed: ☐ Oath ☐ Acknowledgment ☐ Jurat ☐ Other:	**Identification:** ☐ I.D Card ☐ Credible Witness ☐ Drivers License ☐ Known Personally ☐ Passport ☐ Other:	**I.D. Number:**	
		Issued By:	
		Issued Date:	**Expiration Date:**
Document Type:	**Date/Time Notarized:** AM PM	**Document Date:**	**Fee Charged:**

Printed Name and Address of Witness:	**Phone Number:**
	Email:
	Witness' Signature:
Comments :	**Record Number:**

NOTARY RECORD

Printed Name and Address of Signer:	**Phone Number:**	**Thumb Print:**
	Email:	
	Signer's Signature:	

Service Performed: ☐ Oath ☐ Acknowledgment ☐ Jurat ☐ Other:	**Identification:** ☐ I.D Card ☐ Credible Witness ☐ Drivers License ☐ Known Personally ☐ Passport ☐ Other:	**I.D. Number:**	
		Issued By:	
		Issued Date:	**Expiration Date:**
Document Type:	**Date/Time Notarized:** AM PM	**Document Date:**	**Fee Charged:**

Printed Name and Address of Witness:	**Phone Number:**
	Email:
	Witness' Signature:
Comments :	**Record Number:**

NOTARY RECORD

Printed Name and Address of Signer:	**Phone Number:**	**Thumb Print:**
	Email:	
	Signer's Signature:	

Service Performed: ☐ Oath ☐ Acknowledgment ☐ Jurat ☐ Other:	**Identification:** ☐ I.D Card ☐ Credible Witness ☐ Drivers License ☐ Known Personally ☐ Passport ☐ Other:	**I.D. Number:**	
		Issued By:	
		Issued Date:	**Expiration Date:**
Document Type:	**Date/Time Notarized:** AM PM	**Document Date:**	**Fee Charged:**

Printed Name and Address of Witness:	**Phone Number:**
	Email:
	Witness' Signature:
Comments :	**Record Number:**

NOTARY RECORD

Printed Name and Address of Signer:	Phone Number:	Thumb Print:
	Email:	
	Signer's Signature:	

Service Performed:	Identification:		I.D. Number:	
☐ Oath	☐ I.D Card	☐ Credible Witness		
☐ Acknowledgment	☐ Drivers License	☐ Known Personally	Issued By:	
☐ Jurat	☐ Passport			
☐ Other:	☐ Other:		Issued Date:	Expiration Date:
Document Type:	Date/Time Notarized:	AM PM	Document Date:	Fee Charged:

Printed Name and Address of Witness:	Phone Number:
	Email:
	Witness' Signature:

Comments :	Record Number:

NOTARY RECORD

Printed Name and Address of Signer:	Phone Number:	Thumb Print:
	Email:	
	Signer's Signature:	

Service Performed:	Identification:		I.D. Number:	
☐ Oath	☐ I.D Card	☐ Credible Witness		
☐ Acknowledgment	☐ Drivers License	☐ Known Personally	Issued By:	
☐ Jurat	☐ Passport			
☐ Other:	☐ Other:		Issued Date:	Expiration Date:
Document Type:	Date/Time Notarized:	AM PM	Document Date:	Fee Charged:

Printed Name and Address of Witness:	Phone Number:
	Email:
	Witness' Signature:

Comments :	Record Number:

NOTARY RECORD

Printed Name and Address of Signer:	**Phone Number:**	**Thumb Print:**
	Email:	
	Signer's Signature:	

Service Performed: ☐ Oath ☐ Acknowledgment ☐ Jurat ☐ Other:	**Identification:** ☐ I.D Card ☐ Credible Witness ☐ Drivers License ☐ Known Personally ☐ Passport ☐ Other:	**I.D. Number:**	
		Issued By:	
		Issued Date:	**Expiration Date:**
Document Type:	**Date/Time Notarized:** AM PM	**Document Date:**	**Fee Charged:**

Printed Name and Address of Witness:	**Phone Number:**
	Email:
	Witness' Signature:

Comments :	**Record Number:**

NOTARY RECORD

Printed Name and Address of Signer:	**Phone Number:**	**Thumb Print:**
	Email:	
	Signer's Signature:	

Service Performed: ☐ Oath ☐ Acknowledgment ☐ Jurat ☐ Other:	**Identification:** ☐ I.D Card ☐ Credible Witness ☐ Drivers License ☐ Known Personally ☐ Passport ☐ Other:	**I.D. Number:**	
		Issued By:	
		Issued Date:	**Expiration Date:**
Document Type:	**Date/Time Notarized:** AM PM	**Document Date:**	**Fee Charged:**

Printed Name and Address of Witness:	**Phone Number:**
	Email:
	Witness' Signature:

Comments :	**Record Number:**

NOTARY RECORD

Printed Name and Address of Signer:	**Phone Number:**	**Thumb Print:**
	Email:	
	Signer's Signature:	

Service Performed: ☐ Oath ☐ Acknowledgment ☐ Jurat ☐ Other:	**Identification:** ☐ I.D Card ☐ Credible Witness ☐ Drivers License ☐ Known Personally ☐ Passport ☐ Other:	**I.D. Number:**	
		Issued By:	
		Issued Date:	**Expiration Date:**
Document Type:	**Date/Time Notarized:** AM PM	**Document Date:**	**Fee Charged:**

Printed Name and Address of Witness:	**Phone Number:**
	Email:
	Witness' Signature:
Comments :	**Record Number:**

NOTARY RECORD

Printed Name and Address of Signer:	**Phone Number:**	**Thumb Print:**
	Email:	
	Signer's Signature:	

Service Performed: ☐ Oath ☐ Acknowledgment ☐ Jurat ☐ Other:	**Identification:** ☐ I.D Card ☐ Credible Witness ☐ Drivers License ☐ Known Personally ☐ Passport ☐ Other:	**I.D. Number:**	
		Issued By:	
		Issued Date:	**Expiration Date:**
Document Type:	**Date/Time Notarized:** AM PM	**Document Date:**	**Fee Charged:**

Printed Name and Address of Witness:	**Phone Number:**
	Email:
	Witness' Signature:
Comments :	**Record Number:**

NOTARY RECORD

Printed Name and Address of Signer:	**Phone Number:**	**Thumb Print:**
	Email:	
	Signer's Signature:	

Service Performed: ☐ Oath ☐ Acknowledgment ☐ Jurat ☐ Other:	**Identification:** ☐ I.D Card ☐ Credible Witness ☐ Drivers License ☐ Known Personally ☐ Passport ☐ Other:	**I.D. Number:**	
		Issued By:	
		Issued Date:	**Expiration Date:**
Document Type:	**Date/Time Notarized:** AM PM	**Document Date:**	**Fee Charged:**

Printed Name and Address of Witness:	**Phone Number:**
	Email:
	Witness' Signature:

Comments :	**Record Number:**

NOTARY RECORD

Printed Name and Address of Signer:	**Phone Number:**	**Thumb Print:**
	Email:	
	Signer's Signature:	

Service Performed: ☐ Oath ☐ Acknowledgment ☐ Jurat ☐ Other:	**Identification:** ☐ I.D Card ☐ Credible Witness ☐ Drivers License ☐ Known Personally ☐ Passport ☐ Other:	**I.D. Number:**	
		Issued By:	
		Issued Date:	**Expiration Date:**
Document Type:	**Date/Time Notarized:** AM PM	**Document Date:**	**Fee Charged:**

Printed Name and Address of Witness:	**Phone Number:**
	Email:
	Witness' Signature:

Comments :	**Record Number:**

NOTARY RECORD

Printed Name and Address of Signer:	**Phone Number:**	**Thumb Print:**
	Email:	
	Signer's Signature:	

Service Performed: ☐ Oath ☐ Acknowledgment ☐ Jurat ☐ Other:	**Identification:** ☐ I.D Card ☐ Credible Witness ☐ Drivers License ☐ Known Personally ☐ Passport ☐ Other:	**I.D. Number:**	
		Issued By:	
		Issued Date:	**Expiration Date:**
Document Type:	**Date/Time Notarized:** AM PM	**Document Date:**	**Fee Charged:**

Printed Name and Address of Witness:	**Phone Number:**
	Email:
	Witness' Signature:

Comments :	**Record Number:**

NOTARY RECORD

Printed Name and Address of Signer:	**Phone Number:**	**Thumb Print:**
	Email:	
	Signer's Signature:	

Service Performed: ☐ Oath ☐ Acknowledgment ☐ Jurat ☐ Other:	**Identification:** ☐ I.D Card ☐ Credible Witness ☐ Drivers License ☐ Known Personally ☐ Passport ☐ Other:	**I.D. Number:**	
		Issued By:	
		Issued Date:	**Expiration Date:**
Document Type:	**Date/Time Notarized:** AM PM	**Document Date:**	**Fee Charged:**

Printed Name and Address of Witness:	**Phone Number:**
	Email:
	Witness' Signature:

Comments :	**Record Number:**

NOTARY RECORD

Printed Name and Address of Signer:	Phone Number:	Thumb Print:
	Email:	
	Signer's Signature:	

Service Performed:	Identification:		I.D. Number:	
☐ Oath	☐ I.D Card	☐ Credible Witness	Issued By:	
☐ Acknowledgment	☐ Drivers License	☐ Known Personally		
☐ Jurat	☐ Passport		Issued Date:	Expiration Date:
☐ Other:	☐ Other:			
Document Type:	Date/Time Notarized: AM PM		Document Date:	Fee Charged:

Printed Name and Address of Witness:	Phone Number:
	Email:
	Witness' Signature:

Comments :	Record Number:

NOTARY RECORD

Printed Name and Address of Signer:	Phone Number:	Thumb Print:
	Email:	
	Signer's Signature:	

Service Performed:	Identification:		I.D. Number:	
☐ Oath	☐ I.D Card	☐ Credible Witness	Issued By:	
☐ Acknowledgment	☐ Drivers License	☐ Known Personally		
☐ Jurat	☐ Passport		Issued Date:	Expiration Date:
☐ Other:	☐ Other:			
Document Type:	Date/Time Notarized: AM PM		Document Date:	Fee Charged:

Printed Name and Address of Witness:	Phone Number:
	Email:
	Witness' Signature:

Comments :	Record Number:

NOTARY RECORD

Printed Name and Address of Signer:	**Phone Number:**	**Thumb Print:**
	Email:	
	Signer's Signature:	

Service Performed: ☐ Oath ☐ Acknowledgment ☐ Jurat ☐ Other:	**Identification:** ☐ I.D Card ☐ Credible Witness ☐ Drivers License ☐ Known Personally ☐ Passport ☐ Other:	**I.D. Number:**	
		Issued By:	
		Issued Date:	**Expiration Date:**
Document Type:	**Date/Time Notarized:** AM PM	**Document Date:**	**Fee Charged:**

Printed Name and Address of Witness:	**Phone Number:**
	Email:
	Witness' Signature:

Comments :	**Record Number:**

NOTARY RECORD

Printed Name and Address of Signer:	**Phone Number:**	**Thumb Print:**
	Email:	
	Signer's Signature:	

Service Performed: ☐ Oath ☐ Acknowledgment ☐ Jurat ☐ Other:	**Identification:** ☐ I.D Card ☐ Credible Witness ☐ Drivers License ☐ Known Personally ☐ Passport ☐ Other:	**I.D. Number:**	
		Issued By:	
		Issued Date:	**Expiration Date:**
Document Type:	**Date/Time Notarized:** AM PM	**Document Date:**	**Fee Charged:**

Printed Name and Address of Witness:	**Phone Number:**
	Email:
	Witness' Signature:

Comments :	**Record Number:**

NOTARY RECORD

Printed Name and Address of Signer:	**Phone Number:**	**Thumb Print:**
	Email:	
	Signer's Signature:	

Service Performed: ☐ Oath ☐ Acknowledgment ☐ Jurat ☐ Other:	**Identification:** ☐ I.D Card ☐ Credible Witness ☐ Drivers License ☐ Known Personally ☐ Passport ☐ Other:	**I.D. Number:**	
		Issued By:	
		Issued Date:	**Expiration Date:**
Document Type:	**Date/Time Notarized:** AM PM	**Document Date:**	**Fee Charged:**

Printed Name and Address of Witness:	**Phone Number:**
	Email:
	Witness' Signature:
Comments :	**Record Number:**

NOTARY RECORD

Printed Name and Address of Signer:	**Phone Number:**	**Thumb Print:**
	Email:	
	Signer's Signature:	

Service Performed: ☐ Oath ☐ Acknowledgment ☐ Jurat ☐ Other:	**Identification:** ☐ I.D Card ☐ Credible Witness ☐ Drivers License ☐ Known Personally ☐ Passport ☐ Other:	**I.D. Number:**	
		Issued By:	
		Issued Date:	**Expiration Date:**
Document Type:	**Date/Time Notarized:** AM PM	**Document Date:**	**Fee Charged:**

Printed Name and Address of Witness:	**Phone Number:**
	Email:
	Witness' Signature:
Comments :	**Record Number:**

NOTARY RECORD

Printed Name and Address of Signer:	Phone Number:	Thumb Print:
	Email:	
	Signer's Signature:	

Service Performed:	Identification:		I.D. Number:	
☐ Oath	☐ I.D Card	☐ Credible Witness	Issued By:	
☐ Acknowledgment	☐ Drivers License	☐ Known Personally	Issued Date:	Expiration Date:
☐ Jurat	☐ Passport			
☐ Other:	☐ Other:			
Document Type:	Date/Time Notarized:	AM PM	Document Date:	Fee Charged:

Printed Name and Address of Witness:	Phone Number:
	Email:
	Witness' Signature:

Comments :	Record Number:

NOTARY RECORD

Printed Name and Address of Signer:	Phone Number:	Thumb Print:
	Email:	
	Signer's Signature:	

Service Performed:	Identification:		I.D. Number:	
☐ Oath	☐ I.D Card	☐ Credible Witness	Issued By:	
☐ Acknowledgment	☐ Drivers License	☐ Known Personally	Issued Date:	Expiration Date:
☐ Jurat	☐ Passport			
☐ Other:	☐ Other:			
Document Type:	Date/Time Notarized:	AM PM	Document Date:	Fee Charged:

Printed Name and Address of Witness:	Phone Number:
	Email:
	Witness' Signature:

Comments :	Record Number:

NOTARY RECORD

Printed Name and Address of Signer:	Phone Number:	Thumb Print:
	Email:	
	Signer's Signature:	

Service Performed:	Identification:		I.D. Number:	
☐ Oath	☐ I.D Card	☐ Credible Witness	Issued By:	
☐ Acknowledgment	☐ Drivers License	☐ Known Personally		
☐ Jurat	☐ Passport		Issued Date:	Expiration Date:
☐ Other:	☐ Other:			
Document Type:	Date/Time Notarized: AM PM		Document Date:	Fee Charged:

Printed Name and Address of Witness:	Phone Number:
	Email:
	Witness' Signature:

Comments :	Record Number:

NOTARY RECORD

Printed Name and Address of Signer:	Phone Number:	Thumb Print:
	Email:	
	Signer's Signature:	

Service Performed:	Identification:		I.D. Number:	
☐ Oath	☐ I.D Card	☐ Credible Witness	Issued By:	
☐ Acknowledgment	☐ Drivers License	☐ Known Personally		
☐ Jurat	☐ Passport		Issued Date:	Expiration Date:
☐ Other:	☐ Other:			
Document Type:	Date/Time Notarized: AM PM		Document Date:	Fee Charged:

Printed Name and Address of Witness:	Phone Number:
	Email:
	Witness' Signature:

Comments :	Record Number:

NOTARY RECORD

Printed Name and Address of Signer:	**Phone Number:**	**Thumb Print:**
	Email:	
	Signer's Signature:	

Service Performed: ☐ Oath ☐ Acknowledgment ☐ Jurat ☐ Other:	**Identification:** ☐ I.D Card ☐ Credible Witness ☐ Drivers License ☐ Known Personally ☐ Passport ☐ Other:	**I.D. Number:**	
		Issued By:	
		Issued Date:	**Expiration Date:**
Document Type:	**Date/Time Notarized:** AM PM	**Document Date:**	**Fee Charged:**

Printed Name and Address of Witness:	**Phone Number:**
	Email:
	Witness' Signature:
Comments :	**Record Number:**

NOTARY RECORD

Printed Name and Address of Signer:	**Phone Number:**	**Thumb Print:**
	Email:	
	Signer's Signature:	

Service Performed: ☐ Oath ☐ Acknowledgment ☐ Jurat ☐ Other:	**Identification:** ☐ I.D Card ☐ Credible Witness ☐ Drivers License ☐ Known Personally ☐ Passport ☐ Other:	**I.D. Number:**	
		Issued By:	
		Issued Date:	**Expiration Date:**
Document Type:	**Date/Time Notarized:** AM PM	**Document Date:**	**Fee Charged:**

Printed Name and Address of Witness:	**Phone Number:**
	Email:
	Witness' Signature:
Comments :	**Record Number:**

NOTARY RECORD

Printed Name and Address of Signer:	Phone Number:	Thumb Print:
	Email:	
	Signer's Signature:	

Service Performed:	Identification:		I.D. Number:	
☐ Oath	☐ I.D Card	☐ Credible Witness		
☐ Acknowledgment	☐ Drivers License	☐ Known Personally	Issued By:	
☐ Jurat	☐ Passport			
☐ Other:	☐ Other:		Issued Date:	Expiration Date:
Document Type:	Date/Time Notarized:	AM PM	Document Date:	Fee Charged:

Printed Name and Address of Witness:	Phone Number:
	Email:
	Witness' Signature:

Comments :	Record Number:

NOTARY RECORD

Printed Name and Address of Signer:	Phone Number:	Thumb Print:
	Email:	
	Signer's Signature:	

Service Performed:	Identification:		I.D. Number:	
☐ Oath	☐ I.D Card	☐ Credible Witness		
☐ Acknowledgment	☐ Drivers License	☐ Known Personally	Issued By:	
☐ Jurat	☐ Passport			
☐ Other:	☐ Other:		Issued Date:	Expiration Date:
Document Type:	Date/Time Notarized:	AM PM	Document Date:	Fee Charged:

Printed Name and Address of Witness:	Phone Number:
	Email:
	Witness' Signature:

Comments :	Record Number:

NOTARY RECORD

Printed Name and Address of Signer:	**Phone Number:**	**Thumb Print:**
	Email:	
	Signer's Signature:	

Service Performed: ☐ Oath ☐ Acknowledgment ☐ Jurat ☐ Other:	**Identification:** ☐ I.D Card ☐ Credible Witness ☐ Drivers License ☐ Known Personally ☐ Passport ☐ Other:	**I.D. Number:** **Issued By:** **Issued Date:** **Expiration Date:**
Document Type:	**Date/Time Notarized:** AM PM	**Document Date:** **Fee Charged:**

Printed Name and Address of Witness:	**Phone Number:**
	Email:
	Witness' Signature:
Comments :	**Record Number:**

NOTARY RECORD

Printed Name and Address of Signer:	**Phone Number:**	**Thumb Print:**
	Email:	
	Signer's Signature:	

Service Performed: ☐ Oath ☐ Acknowledgment ☐ Jurat ☐ Other:	**Identification:** ☐ I.D Card ☐ Credible Witness ☐ Drivers License ☐ Known Personally ☐ Passport ☐ Other:	**I.D. Number:** **Issued By:** **Issued Date:** **Expiration Date:**
Document Type:	**Date/Time Notarized:** AM PM	**Document Date:** **Fee Charged:**

Printed Name and Address of Witness:	**Phone Number:**
	Email:
	Witness' Signature:
Comments :	**Record Number:**

NOTARY RECORD

Printed Name and Address of Signer:	**Phone Number:**	**Thumb Print:**
	Email:	
	Signer's Signature:	

Service Performed: ☐ Oath ☐ Acknowledgment ☐ Jurat ☐ Other:	**Identification:** ☐ I.D Card ☐ Credible Witness ☐ Drivers License ☐ Known Personally ☐ Passport ☐ Other:	**I.D. Number:**	
		Issued By:	
		Issued Date:	**Expiration Date:**
Document Type:	**Date/Time Notarized:** AM PM	**Document Date:**	**Fee Charged:**

Printed Name and Address of Witness:	**Phone Number:**
	Email:
	Witness' Signature:
Comments :	**Record Number:**

NOTARY RECORD

Printed Name and Address of Signer:	**Phone Number:**	**Thumb Print:**
	Email:	
	Signer's Signature:	

Service Performed: ☐ Oath ☐ Acknowledgment ☐ Jurat ☐ Other:	**Identification:** ☐ I.D Card ☐ Credible Witness ☐ Drivers License ☐ Known Personally ☐ Passport ☐ Other:	**I.D. Number:**	
		Issued By:	
		Issued Date:	**Expiration Date:**
Document Type:	**Date/Time Notarized:** AM PM	**Document Date:**	**Fee Charged:**

Printed Name and Address of Witness:	**Phone Number:**
	Email:
	Witness' Signature:
Comments :	**Record Number:**

NOTARY RECORD

Printed Name and Address of Signer:	Phone Number:	Thumb Print:
	Email:	
	Signer's Signature:	

Service Performed:	Identification:		I.D. Number:	
☐ Oath	☐ I.D Card	☐ Credible Witness		
☐ Acknowledgment	☐ Drivers License	☐ Known Personally	Issued By:	
☐ Jurat	☐ Passport			
☐ Other:	☐ Other:		Issued Date:	Expiration Date:
Document Type:	Date/Time Notarized: AM PM		Document Date:	Fee Charged:

Printed Name and Address of Witness:	Phone Number:
	Email:
	Witness' Signature:

Comments :	Record Number:

NOTARY RECORD

Printed Name and Address of Signer:	Phone Number:	Thumb Print:
	Email:	
	Signer's Signature:	

Service Performed:	Identification:		I.D. Number:	
☐ Oath	☐ I.D Card	☐ Credible Witness		
☐ Acknowledgment	☐ Drivers License	☐ Known Personally	Issued By:	
☐ Jurat	☐ Passport			
☐ Other:	☐ Other:		Issued Date:	Expiration Date:
Document Type:	Date/Time Notarized: AM PM		Document Date:	Fee Charged:

Printed Name and Address of Witness:	Phone Number:
	Email:
	Witness' Signature:

Comments :	Record Number:

NOTARY RECORD

Printed Name and Address of Signer:

Phone Number:

Email:

Signer's Signature:

Thumb Print:

Service Performed:

- ☐ Oath
- ☐ Acknowledgment
- ☐ Jurat
- ☐ Other:

Identification:

- ☐ I.D Card
- ☐ Credible Witness
- ☐ Drivers License
- ☐ Known Personally
- ☐ Passport
- ☐ Other:

I.D. Number:

Issued By:

Issued Date:

Expiration Date:

Document Type:

Date/Time Notarized: AM PM

Document Date:

Fee Charged:

Printed Name and Address of Witness:

Phone Number:

Email:

Witness' Signature:

Comments :

Record Number:

NOTARY RECORD

Printed Name and Address of Signer:

Phone Number:

Email:

Signer's Signature:

Thumb Print:

Service Performed:

- ☐ Oath
- ☐ Acknowledgment
- ☐ Jurat
- ☐ Other:

Identification:

- ☐ I.D Card
- ☐ Credible Witness
- ☐ Drivers License
- ☐ Known Personally
- ☐ Passport
- ☐ Other:

I.D. Number:

Issued By:

Issued Date:

Expiration Date:

Document Type:

Date/Time Notarized: AM PM

Document Date:

Fee Charged:

Printed Name and Address of Witness:

Phone Number:

Email:

Witness' Signature:

Comments :

Record Number:

NOTARY RECORD

Printed Name and Address of Signer:	Phone Number:	Thumb Print:
	Email:	
	Signer's Signature:	

Service Performed:	Identification:		I.D. Number:	
☐ Oath	☐ I.D Card	☐ Credible Witness	Issued By:	
☐ Acknowledgment	☐ Drivers License	☐ Known Personally	Issued Date:	Expiration Date:
☐ Jurat	☐ Passport			
☐ Other:	☐ Other:			
Document Type:	Date/Time Notarized:	AM PM	Document Date:	Fee Charged:

Printed Name and Address of Witness:	Phone Number:
	Email:
	Witness' Signature:

Comments :	Record Number:

NOTARY RECORD

Printed Name and Address of Signer:	Phone Number:	Thumb Print:
	Email:	
	Signer's Signature:	

Service Performed:	Identification:		I.D. Number:	
☐ Oath	☐ I.D Card	☐ Credible Witness	Issued By:	
☐ Acknowledgment	☐ Drivers License	☐ Known Personally	Issued Date:	Expiration Date:
☐ Jurat	☐ Passport			
☐ Other:	☐ Other:			
Document Type:	Date/Time Notarized:	AM PM	Document Date:	Fee Charged:

Printed Name and Address of Witness:	Phone Number:
	Email:
	Witness' Signature:

Comments :	Record Number:

NOTARY RECORD

Printed Name and Address of Signer:	Phone Number:	Thumb Print:
	Email:	
	Signer's Signature:	

Service Performed:	Identification:		I.D. Number:	
☐ Oath	☐ I.D Card	☐ Credible Witness		
☐ Acknowledgment	☐ Drivers License	☐ Known Personally	Issued By:	
☐ Jurat	☐ Passport			
☐ Other:	☐ Other:		Issued Date:	Expiration Date:
Document Type:	Date/Time Notarized: AM PM		Document Date:	Fee Charged:

Printed Name and Address of Witness:	Phone Number:
	Email:
	Witness' Signature:

Comments :	Record Number:

NOTARY RECORD

Printed Name and Address of Signer:	Phone Number:	Thumb Print:
	Email:	
	Signer's Signature:	

Service Performed:	Identification:		I.D. Number:	
☐ Oath	☐ I.D Card	☐ Credible Witness		
☐ Acknowledgment	☐ Drivers License	☐ Known Personally	Issued By:	
☐ Jurat	☐ Passport			
☐ Other:	☐ Other:		Issued Date:	Expiration Date:
Document Type:	Date/Time Notarized: AM PM		Document Date:	Fee Charged:

Printed Name and Address of Witness:	Phone Number:
	Email:
	Witness' Signature:

Comments :	Record Number:

NOTARY RECORD

Printed Name and Address of Signer:	**Phone Number:**	**Thumb Print:**
	Email:	
	Signer's Signature:	

Service Performed: ☐ Oath ☐ Acknowledgment ☐ Jurat ☐ Other:	**Identification:** ☐ I.D Card ☐ Credible Witness ☐ Drivers License ☐ Known Personally ☐ Passport ☐ Other:	**I.D. Number:**	
		Issued By:	
		Issued Date:	**Expiration Date:**
Document Type:	**Date/Time Notarized:** AM PM	**Document Date:**	**Fee Charged:**

Printed Name and Address of Witness:	**Phone Number:**
	Email:
	Witness' Signature:
Comments :	**Record Number:**

NOTARY RECORD

Printed Name and Address of Signer:	**Phone Number:**	**Thumb Print:**
	Email:	
	Signer's Signature:	

Service Performed: ☐ Oath ☐ Acknowledgment ☐ Jurat ☐ Other:	**Identification:** ☐ I.D Card ☐ Credible Witness ☐ Drivers License ☐ Known Personally ☐ Passport ☐ Other:	**I.D. Number:**	
		Issued By:	
		Issued Date:	**Expiration Date:**
Document Type:	**Date/Time Notarized:** AM PM	**Document Date:**	**Fee Charged:**

Printed Name and Address of Witness:	**Phone Number:**
	Email:
	Witness' Signature:
Comments :	**Record Number:**

NOTARY RECORD

Printed Name and Address of Signer:	**Phone Number:**	**Thumb Print:**
	Email:	
	Signer's Signature:	

Service Performed: ☐ Oath ☐ Acknowledgment ☐ Jurat ☐ Other:	**Identification:** ☐ I.D Card ☐ Credible Witness ☐ Drivers License ☐ Known Personally ☐ Passport ☐ Other:	**I.D. Number:**	
		Issued By:	
		Issued Date:	**Expiration Date:**
Document Type:	**Date/Time Notarized:** AM PM	**Document Date:**	**Fee Charged:**

Printed Name and Address of Witness:	**Phone Number:**
	Email:
	Witness' Signature:
Comments :	**Record Number:**

NOTARY RECORD

Printed Name and Address of Signer:	**Phone Number:**	**Thumb Print:**
	Email:	
	Signer's Signature:	

Service Performed: ☐ Oath ☐ Acknowledgment ☐ Jurat ☐ Other:	**Identification:** ☐ I.D Card ☐ Credible Witness ☐ Drivers License ☐ Known Personally ☐ Passport ☐ Other:	**I.D. Number:**	
		Issued By:	
		Issued Date:	**Expiration Date:**
Document Type:	**Date/Time Notarized:** AM PM	**Document Date:**	**Fee Charged:**

Printed Name and Address of Witness:	**Phone Number:**
	Email:
	Witness' Signature:
Comments :	**Record Number:**

NOTARY RECORD

Printed Name and Address of Signer:	Phone Number:	Thumb Print:
	Email:	
	Signer's Signature:	

Service Performed:	Identification:		I.D. Number:	
☐ Oath	☐ I.D Card	☐ Credible Witness	Issued By:	
☐ Acknowledgment	☐ Drivers License	☐ Known Personally		
☐ Jurat	☐ Passport		Issued Date:	Expiration Date:
☐ Other:	☐ Other:			
Document Type:	Date/Time Notarized:	AM PM	Document Date:	Fee Charged:

Printed Name and Address of Witness:	Phone Number:
	Email:
	Witness' Signature:

Comments :	Record Number:

NOTARY RECORD

Printed Name and Address of Signer:	Phone Number:	Thumb Print:
	Email:	
	Signer's Signature:	

Service Performed:	Identification:		I.D. Number:	
☐ Oath	☐ I.D Card	☐ Credible Witness	Issued By:	
☐ Acknowledgment	☐ Drivers License	☐ Known Personally		
☐ Jurat	☐ Passport		Issued Date:	Expiration Date:
☐ Other:	☐ Other:			
Document Type:	Date/Time Notarized:	AM PM	Document Date:	Fee Charged:

Printed Name and Address of Witness:	Phone Number:
	Email:
	Witness' Signature:

Comments :	Record Number:

NOTARY RECORD

Printed Name and Address of Signer:	Phone Number:	Thumb Print:
	Email:	
	Signer's Signature:	

Service Performed:	Identification:		I.D. Number:	
☐ Oath	☐ I.D Card	☐ Credible Witness	Issued By:	
☐ Acknowledgment	☐ Drivers License	☐ Known Personally		
☐ Jurat	☐ Passport		Issued Date:	Expiration Date:
☐ Other:	☐ Other:			
Document Type:	Date/Time Notarized: AM PM		Document Date:	Fee Charged:

Printed Name and Address of Witness:	Phone Number:
	Email:
	Witness' Signature:

Comments :	Record Number:

NOTARY RECORD

Printed Name and Address of Signer:	Phone Number:	Thumb Print:
	Email:	
	Signer's Signature:	

Service Performed:	Identification:		I.D. Number:	
☐ Oath	☐ I.D Card	☐ Credible Witness	Issued By:	
☐ Acknowledgment	☐ Drivers License	☐ Known Personally		
☐ Jurat	☐ Passport		Issued Date:	Expiration Date:
☐ Other:	☐ Other:			
Document Type:	Date/Time Notarized: AM PM		Document Date:	Fee Charged:

Printed Name and Address of Witness:	Phone Number:
	Email:
	Witness' Signature:

Comments :	Record Number:

NOTARY RECORD

Printed Name and Address of Signer:	**Phone Number:**	**Thumb Print:**
	Email:	
	Signer's Signature:	

Service Performed: ☐ Oath ☐ Acknowledgment ☐ Jurat ☐ Other:	**Identification:** ☐ I.D Card ☐ Credible Witness ☐ Drivers License ☐ Known Personally ☐ Passport ☐ Other:	**I.D. Number:**	
		Issued By:	
		Issued Date:	**Expiration Date:**
Document Type:	**Date/Time Notarized:** AM PM	**Document Date:**	**Fee Charged:**

Printed Name and Address of Witness:	**Phone Number:**
	Email:
	Witness' Signature:
Comments :	**Record Number:**

NOTARY RECORD

Printed Name and Address of Signer:	**Phone Number:**	**Thumb Print:**
	Email:	
	Signer's Signature:	

Service Performed: ☐ Oath ☐ Acknowledgment ☐ Jurat ☐ Other:	**Identification:** ☐ I.D Card ☐ Credible Witness ☐ Drivers License ☐ Known Personally ☐ Passport ☐ Other:	**I.D. Number:**	
		Issued By:	
		Issued Date:	**Expiration Date:**
Document Type:	**Date/Time Notarized:** AM PM	**Document Date:**	**Fee Charged:**

Printed Name and Address of Witness:	**Phone Number:**
	Email:
	Witness' Signature:
Comments :	**Record Number:**

NOTARY RECORD

Printed Name and Address of Signer:	**Phone Number:**	**Thumb Print:**
	Email:	
	Signer's Signature:	

Service Performed: ☐ Oath ☐ Acknowledgment ☐ Jurat ☐ Other:	**Identification:** ☐ I.D Card ☐ Credible Witness ☐ Drivers License ☐ Known Personally ☐ Passport ☐ Other:	**I.D. Number:**	
		Issued By:	
		Issued Date:	**Expiration Date:**
Document Type:	**Date/Time Notarized:** AM PM	**Document Date:**	**Fee Charged:**

Printed Name and Address of Witness:	**Phone Number:**
	Email:
	Witness' Signature:
Comments :	**Record Number:**

NOTARY RECORD

Printed Name and Address of Signer:	**Phone Number:**	**Thumb Print:**
	Email:	
	Signer's Signature:	

Service Performed: ☐ Oath ☐ Acknowledgment ☐ Jurat ☐ Other:	**Identification:** ☐ I.D Card ☐ Credible Witness ☐ Drivers License ☐ Known Personally ☐ Passport ☐ Other:	**I.D. Number:**	
		Issued By:	
		Issued Date:	**Expiration Date:**
Document Type:	**Date/Time Notarized:** AM PM	**Document Date:**	**Fee Charged:**

Printed Name and Address of Witness:	**Phone Number:**
	Email:
	Witness' Signature:
Comments :	**Record Number:**

NOTARY RECORD

Printed Name and Address of Signer:	Phone Number:	Thumb Print:
	Email:	
	Signer's Signature:	

Service Performed:	Identification:		I.D. Number:	
☐ Oath	☐ I.D Card	☐ Credible Witness	Issued By:	
☐ Acknowledgment	☐ Drivers License	☐ Known Personally		
☐ Jurat	☐ Passport		Issued Date:	Expiration Date:
☐ Other:	☐ Other:			
Document Type:	Date/Time Notarized: AM PM		Document Date:	Fee Charged:

Printed Name and Address of Witness:	Phone Number:
	Email:
	Witness' Signature:

Comments :	Record Number:

NOTARY RECORD

Printed Name and Address of Signer:	Phone Number:	Thumb Print:
	Email:	
	Signer's Signature:	

Service Performed:	Identification:		I.D. Number:	
☐ Oath	☐ I.D Card	☐ Credible Witness	Issued By:	
☐ Acknowledgment	☐ Drivers License	☐ Known Personally		
☐ Jurat	☐ Passport		Issued Date:	Expiration Date:
☐ Other:	☐ Other:			
Document Type:	Date/Time Notarized: AM PM		Document Date:	Fee Charged:

Printed Name and Address of Witness:	Phone Number:
	Email:
	Witness' Signature:

Comments :	Record Number:

NOTARY RECORD

Printed Name and Address of Signer:	Phone Number:	Thumb Print:
	Email:	
	Signer's Signature:	

Service Performed:	Identification:		I.D. Number:	
☐ Oath	☐ I.D Card	☐ Credible Witness	Issued By:	
☐ Acknowledgment	☐ Drivers License	☐ Known Personally	Issued Date:	Expiration Date:
☐ Jurat	☐ Passport			
☐ Other:	☐ Other:			
Document Type:	Date/Time Notarized: AM PM		Document Date:	Fee Charged:

Printed Name and Address of Witness:	Phone Number:
	Email:
	Witness' Signature:

Comments :	Record Number:

NOTARY RECORD

Printed Name and Address of Signer:	Phone Number:	Thumb Print:
	Email:	
	Signer's Signature:	

Service Performed:	Identification:		I.D. Number:	
☐ Oath	☐ I.D Card	☐ Credible Witness	Issued By:	
☐ Acknowledgment	☐ Drivers License	☐ Known Personally	Issued Date:	Expiration Date:
☐ Jurat	☐ Passport			
☐ Other:	☐ Other:			
Document Type:	Date/Time Notarized: AM PM		Document Date:	Fee Charged:

Printed Name and Address of Witness:	Phone Number:
	Email:
	Witness' Signature:

Comments :	Record Number:

NOTARY RECORD

Printed Name and Address of Signer:	Phone Number:	Thumb Print:
	Email:	
	Signer's Signature:	

Service Performed:	Identification:		I.D. Number:	
☐ Oath	☐ I.D Card	☐ Credible Witness	Issued By:	
☐ Acknowledgment	☐ Drivers License	☐ Known Personally		
☐ Jurat	☐ Passport		Issued Date:	Expiration Date:
☐ Other:	☐ Other:			
Document Type:	Date/Time Notarized:	AM PM	Document Date:	Fee Charged:

Printed Name and Address of Witness:	Phone Number:
	Email:
	Witness' Signature:

Comments :	Record Number:

NOTARY RECORD

Printed Name and Address of Signer:	Phone Number:	Thumb Print:
	Email:	
	Signer's Signature:	

Service Performed:	Identification:		I.D. Number:	
☐ Oath	☐ I.D Card	☐ Credible Witness	Issued By:	
☐ Acknowledgment	☐ Drivers License	☐ Known Personally		
☐ Jurat	☐ Passport		Issued Date:	Expiration Date:
☐ Other:	☐ Other:			
Document Type:	Date/Time Notarized:	AM PM	Document Date:	Fee Charged:

Printed Name and Address of Witness:	Phone Number:
	Email:
	Witness' Signature:

Comments :	Record Number:

NOTARY RECORD

Printed Name and Address of Signer:	Phone Number:	Thumb Print:
	Email:	
	Signer's Signature:	

Service Performed:	Identification:		I.D. Number:	
☐ Oath	☐ I.D Card	☐ Credible Witness	Issued By:	
☐ Acknowledgment	☐ Drivers License	☐ Known Personally	Issued Date:	Expiration Date:
☐ Jurat	☐ Passport			
☐ Other:	☐ Other:			
Document Type:	Date/Time Notarized: AM PM		Document Date:	Fee Charged:

Printed Name and Address of Witness:	Phone Number:
	Email:
	Witness' Signature:

Comments :	Record Number:

NOTARY RECORD

Printed Name and Address of Signer:	Phone Number:	Thumb Print:
	Email:	
	Signer's Signature:	

Service Performed:	Identification:		I.D. Number:	
☐ Oath	☐ I.D Card	☐ Credible Witness	Issued By:	
☐ Acknowledgment	☐ Drivers License	☐ Known Personally	Issued Date:	Expiration Date:
☐ Jurat	☐ Passport			
☐ Other:	☐ Other:			
Document Type:	Date/Time Notarized: AM PM		Document Date:	Fee Charged:

Printed Name and Address of Witness:	Phone Number:
	Email:
	Witness' Signature:

Comments :	Record Number:

NOTARY RECORD

Printed Name and Address of Signer:	**Phone Number:**	**Thumb Print:**
	Email:	
	Signer's Signature:	

Service Performed: ☐ Oath ☐ Acknowledgment ☐ Jurat ☐ Other:	**Identification:** ☐ I.D Card ☐ Credible Witness ☐ Drivers License ☐ Known Personally ☐ Passport ☐ Other:	**I.D. Number:**	
		Issued By:	
		Issued Date:	**Expiration Date:**
Document Type:	**Date/Time Notarized:** AM PM	**Document Date:**	**Fee Charged:**

Printed Name and Address of Witness:	**Phone Number:**
	Email:
	Witness' Signature:

Comments :	**Record Number:**

NOTARY RECORD

Printed Name and Address of Signer:	**Phone Number:**	**Thumb Print:**
	Email:	
	Signer's Signature:	

Service Performed: ☐ Oath ☐ Acknowledgment ☐ Jurat ☐ Other:	**Identification:** ☐ I.D Card ☐ Credible Witness ☐ Drivers License ☐ Known Personally ☐ Passport ☐ Other:	**I.D. Number:**	
		Issued By:	
		Issued Date:	**Expiration Date:**
Document Type:	**Date/Time Notarized:** AM PM	**Document Date:**	**Fee Charged:**

Printed Name and Address of Witness:	**Phone Number:**
	Email:
	Witness' Signature:

Comments :	**Record Number:**

NOTARY RECORD

Printed Name and Address of Signer:	**Phone Number:**	**Thumb Print:**
	Email:	
	Signer's Signature:	

Service Performed: ☐ Oath ☐ Acknowledgment ☐ Jurat ☐ Other:	**Identification:** ☐ I.D Card ☐ Credible Witness ☐ Drivers License ☐ Known Personally ☐ Passport ☐ Other:	**I.D. Number:**	
		Issued By:	
		Issued Date:	**Expiration Date:**
Document Type:	**Date/Time Notarized:** AM PM	**Document Date:**	**Fee Charged:**

Printed Name and Address of Witness:	**Phone Number:**
	Email:
	Witness' Signature:

Comments :	**Record Number:**

NOTARY RECORD

Printed Name and Address of Signer:	**Phone Number:**	**Thumb Print:**
	Email:	
	Signer's Signature:	

Service Performed: ☐ Oath ☐ Acknowledgment ☐ Jurat ☐ Other:	**Identification:** ☐ I.D Card ☐ Credible Witness ☐ Drivers License ☐ Known Personally ☐ Passport ☐ Other:	**I.D. Number:**	
		Issued By:	
		Issued Date:	**Expiration Date:**
Document Type:	**Date/Time Notarized:** AM PM	**Document Date:**	**Fee Charged:**

Printed Name and Address of Witness:	**Phone Number:**
	Email:
	Witness' Signature:

Comments :	**Record Number:**

NOTARY RECORD

Printed Name and Address of Signer:	**Phone Number:**	**Thumb Print:**
	Email:	
	Signer's Signature:	

Service Performed: ☐ Oath ☐ Acknowledgment ☐ Jurat ☐ Other:	**Identification:** ☐ I.D Card ☐ Credible Witness ☐ Drivers License ☐ Known Personally ☐ Passport ☐ Other:	**I.D. Number:**	
		Issued By:	
		Issued Date:	**Expiration Date:**
Document Type:	**Date/Time Notarized:** AM PM	**Document Date:**	**Fee Charged:**

Printed Name and Address of Witness:	**Phone Number:**
	Email:
	Witness' Signature:
Comments :	**Record Number:**

NOTARY RECORD

Printed Name and Address of Signer:	**Phone Number:**	**Thumb Print:**
	Email:	
	Signer's Signature:	

Service Performed: ☐ Oath ☐ Acknowledgment ☐ Jurat ☐ Other:	**Identification:** ☐ I.D Card ☐ Credible Witness ☐ Drivers License ☐ Known Personally ☐ Passport ☐ Other:	**I.D. Number:**	
		Issued By:	
		Issued Date:	**Expiration Date:**
Document Type:	**Date/Time Notarized:** AM PM	**Document Date:**	**Fee Charged:**

Printed Name and Address of Witness:	**Phone Number:**
	Email:
	Witness' Signature:
Comments :	**Record Number:**

NOTARY RECORD

Printed Name and Address of Signer:	**Phone Number:**	**Thumb Print:**
	Email:	
	Signer's Signature:	

Service Performed: ☐ Oath ☐ Acknowledgment ☐ Jurat ☐ Other:	**Identification:** ☐ I.D Card ☐ Credible Witness ☐ Drivers License ☐ Known Personally ☐ Passport ☐ Other:	**I.D. Number:**	
		Issued By:	
		Issued Date:	**Expiration Date:**
Document Type:	**Date/Time Notarized:** AM PM	**Document Date:**	**Fee Charged:**

Printed Name and Address of Witness:	**Phone Number:**
	Email:
	Witness' Signature:

Comments :	**Record Number:**

NOTARY RECORD

Printed Name and Address of Signer:	**Phone Number:**	**Thumb Print:**
	Email:	
	Signer's Signature:	

Service Performed: ☐ Oath ☐ Acknowledgment ☐ Jurat ☐ Other:	**Identification:** ☐ I.D Card ☐ Credible Witness ☐ Drivers License ☐ Known Personally ☐ Passport ☐ Other:	**I.D. Number:**	
		Issued By:	
		Issued Date:	**Expiration Date:**
Document Type:	**Date/Time Notarized:** AM PM	**Document Date:**	**Fee Charged:**

Printed Name and Address of Witness:	**Phone Number:**
	Email:
	Witness' Signature:

Comments :	**Record Number:**

NOTARY RECORD

Printed Name and Address of Signer:

Phone Number:

Email:

Signer's Signature:

Thumb Print:

Service Performed:

- ☐ Oath
- ☐ Acknowledgment
- ☐ Jurat
- ☐ Other:

Identification:

- ☐ I.D Card
- ☐ Credible Witness
- ☐ Drivers License
- ☐ Known Personally
- ☐ Passport
- ☐ Other:

I.D. Number:

Issued By:

Issued Date:

Expiration Date:

Document Type:

Date/Time Notarized: AM PM

Document Date:

Fee Charged:

Printed Name and Address of Witness:

Phone Number:

Email:

Witness' Signature:

Comments :

Record Number:

NOTARY RECORD

Printed Name and Address of Signer:

Phone Number:

Email:

Signer's Signature:

Thumb Print:

Service Performed:

- ☐ Oath
- ☐ Acknowledgment
- ☐ Jurat
- ☐ Other:

Identification:

- ☐ I.D Card
- ☐ Credible Witness
- ☐ Drivers License
- ☐ Known Personally
- ☐ Passport
- ☐ Other:

I.D. Number:

Issued By:

Issued Date:

Expiration Date:

Document Type:

Date/Time Notarized: AM PM

Document Date:

Fee Charged:

Printed Name and Address of Witness:

Phone Number:

Email:

Witness' Signature:

Comments :

Record Number:

NOTARY RECORD

Printed Name and Address of Signer:	Phone Number:	Thumb Print:
	Email:	
	Signer's Signature:	

Service Performed:	Identification:		I.D. Number:	
☐ Oath	☐ I.D Card	☐ Credible Witness	Issued By:	
☐ Acknowledgment	☐ Drivers License	☐ Known Personally		
☐ Jurat	☐ Passport			
☐ Other:	☐ Other:		Issued Date:	Expiration Date:
Document Type:	Date/Time Notarized: AM PM		Document Date:	Fee Charged:

Printed Name and Address of Witness:	Phone Number:
	Email:
	Witness' Signature:

Comments :	Record Number:

NOTARY RECORD

Printed Name and Address of Signer:	Phone Number:	Thumb Print:
	Email:	
	Signer's Signature:	

Service Performed:	Identification:		I.D. Number:	
☐ Oath	☐ I.D Card	☐ Credible Witness	Issued By:	
☐ Acknowledgment	☐ Drivers License	☐ Known Personally		
☐ Jurat	☐ Passport			
☐ Other:	☐ Other:		Issued Date:	Expiration Date:
Document Type:	Date/Time Notarized: AM PM		Document Date:	Fee Charged:

Printed Name and Address of Witness:	Phone Number:
	Email:
	Witness' Signature:

Comments :	Record Number:

NOTARY RECORD

Printed Name and Address of Signer:	**Phone Number:** **Email:** **Signer's Signature:**	**Thumb Print:**

Service Performed: ☐ Oath ☐ Acknowledgment ☐ Jurat ☐ Other:	**Identification:** ☐ I.D Card ☐ Credible Witness ☐ Drivers License ☐ Known Personally ☐ Passport ☐ Other:	**I.D. Number:** **Issued By:** **Issued Date:**	 **Expiration Date:**
Document Type:	**Date/Time Notarized:** **AM** **PM**	**Document Date:**	**Fee Charged:**

Printed Name and Address of Witness:	**Phone Number:** **Email:** **Witness' Signature:**
Comments :	**Record Number:**

NOTARY RECORD

Printed Name and Address of Signer:	**Phone Number:** **Email:** **Signer's Signature:**	**Thumb Print:**

Service Performed: ☐ Oath ☐ Acknowledgment ☐ Jurat ☐ Other:	**Identification:** ☐ I.D Card ☐ Credible Witness ☐ Drivers License ☐ Known Personally ☐ Passport ☐ Other:	**I.D. Number:** **Issued By:** **Issued Date:**	 **Expiration Date:**
Document Type:	**Date/Time Notarized:** **AM** **PM**	**Document Date:**	**Fee Charged:**

Printed Name and Address of Witness:	**Phone Number:** **Email:** **Witness' Signature:**
Comments :	**Record Number:**

NOTARY RECORD

Printed Name and Address of Signer:	**Phone Number:**	**Thumb Print:**
	Email:	
	Signer's Signature:	

Service Performed: ☐ Oath ☐ Acknowledgment ☐ Jurat ☐ Other:	**Identification:** ☐ I.D Card ☐ Credible Witness ☐ Drivers License ☐ Known Personally ☐ Passport ☐ Other:	**I.D. Number:**	
		Issued By:	
		Issued Date:	**Expiration Date:**
Document Type:	**Date/Time Notarized:** AM PM	**Document Date:**	**Fee Charged:**

Printed Name and Address of Witness:	**Phone Number:**
	Email:
	Witness' Signature:

Comments :	**Record Number:**

NOTARY RECORD

Printed Name and Address of Signer:	**Phone Number:**	**Thumb Print:**
	Email:	
	Signer's Signature:	

Service Performed: ☐ Oath ☐ Acknowledgment ☐ Jurat ☐ Other:	**Identification:** ☐ I.D Card ☐ Credible Witness ☐ Drivers License ☐ Known Personally ☐ Passport ☐ Other:	**I.D. Number:**	
		Issued By:	
		Issued Date:	**Expiration Date:**
Document Type:	**Date/Time Notarized:** AM PM	**Document Date:**	**Fee Charged:**

Printed Name and Address of Witness:	**Phone Number:**
	Email:
	Witness' Signature:

Comments :	**Record Number:**

NOTARY RECORD

Printed Name and Address of Signer:	**Phone Number:**	**Thumb Print:**
	Email:	
	Signer's Signature:	

Service Performed: ☐ Oath ☐ Acknowledgment ☐ Jurat ☐ Other:	**Identification:** ☐ I.D Card ☐ Credible Witness ☐ Drivers License ☐ Known Personally ☐ Passport ☐ Other:	**I.D. Number:**	
		Issued By:	
		Issued Date:	**Expiration Date:**
Document Type:	**Date/Time Notarized:** AM PM	**Document Date:**	**Fee Charged:**

Printed Name and Address of Witness:	**Phone Number:**
	Email:
	Witness' Signature:
Comments :	**Record Number:**

NOTARY RECORD

Printed Name and Address of Signer:	**Phone Number:**	**Thumb Print:**
	Email:	
	Signer's Signature:	

Service Performed: ☐ Oath ☐ Acknowledgment ☐ Jurat ☐ Other:	**Identification:** ☐ I.D Card ☐ Credible Witness ☐ Drivers License ☐ Known Personally ☐ Passport ☐ Other:	**I.D. Number:**	
		Issued By:	
		Issued Date:	**Expiration Date:**
Document Type:	**Date/Time Notarized:** AM PM	**Document Date:**	**Fee Charged:**

Printed Name and Address of Witness:	**Phone Number:**
	Email:
	Witness' Signature:
Comments :	**Record Number:**

NOTARY RECORD

Printed Name and Address of Signer:	**Phone Number:**	**Thumb Print:**
	Email:	
	Signer's Signature:	

Service Performed: ☐ Oath ☐ Acknowledgment ☐ Jurat ☐ Other:	**Identification:** ☐ I.D Card ☐ Credible Witness ☐ Drivers License ☐ Known Personally ☐ Passport ☐ Other:	**I.D. Number:**	
		Issued By:	
		Issued Date:	**Expiration Date:**
Document Type:	**Date/Time Notarized:** AM PM	**Document Date:**	**Fee Charged:**

Printed Name and Address of Witness:	**Phone Number:**
	Email:
	Witness' Signature:

Comments :	**Record Number:**

NOTARY RECORD

Printed Name and Address of Signer:	**Phone Number:**	**Thumb Print:**
	Email:	
	Signer's Signature:	

Service Performed: ☐ Oath ☐ Acknowledgment ☐ Jurat ☐ Other:	**Identification:** ☐ I.D Card ☐ Credible Witness ☐ Drivers License ☐ Known Personally ☐ Passport ☐ Other:	**I.D. Number:**	
		Issued By:	
		Issued Date:	**Expiration Date:**
Document Type:	**Date/Time Notarized:** AM PM	**Document Date:**	**Fee Charged:**

Printed Name and Address of Witness:	**Phone Number:**
	Email:
	Witness' Signature:

Comments :	**Record Number:**

NOTARY RECORD

Printed Name and Address of Signer:	Phone Number:	Thumb Print:
	Email:	
	Signer's Signature:	

Service Performed:	Identification:		I.D. Number:	
☐ Oath	☐ I.D Card	☐ Credible Witness	Issued By:	
☐ Acknowledgment	☐ Drivers License	☐ Known Personally		
☐ Jurat	☐ Passport		Issued Date:	Expiration Date:
☐ Other:	☐ Other:			
Document Type:	Date/Time Notarized:	AM PM	Document Date:	Fee Charged:

Printed Name and Address of Witness:	Phone Number:
	Email:
	Witness' Signature:

Comments :	Record Number:

NOTARY RECORD

Printed Name and Address of Signer:	Phone Number:	Thumb Print:
	Email:	
	Signer's Signature:	

Service Performed:	Identification:		I.D. Number:	
☐ Oath	☐ I.D Card	☐ Credible Witness	Issued By:	
☐ Acknowledgment	☐ Drivers License	☐ Known Personally		
☐ Jurat	☐ Passport		Issued Date:	Expiration Date:
☐ Other:	☐ Other:			
Document Type:	Date/Time Notarized:	AM PM	Document Date:	Fee Charged:

Printed Name and Address of Witness:	Phone Number:
	Email:
	Witness' Signature:

Comments :	Record Number:

NOTARY RECORD

Printed Name and Address of Signer:

Phone Number:

Email:

Signer's Signature:

Thumb Print:

Service Performed:

- ☐ Oath
- ☐ Acknowledgment
- ☐ Jurat
- ☐ Other:

Identification:

- ☐ I.D Card
- ☐ Credible Witness
- ☐ Drivers License
- ☐ Known Personally
- ☐ Passport
- ☐ Other:

I.D. Number:

Issued By:

Issued Date:

Expiration Date:

Document Type:

Date/Time Notarized: **AM** **PM**

Document Date:

Fee Charged:

Printed Name and Address of Witness:

Phone Number:

Email:

Witness' Signature:

Comments :

Record Number:

NOTARY RECORD

Printed Name and Address of Signer:

Phone Number:

Email:

Signer's Signature:

Thumb Print:

Service Performed:

- ☐ Oath
- ☐ Acknowledgment
- ☐ Jurat
- ☐ Other:

Identification:

- ☐ I.D Card
- ☐ Credible Witness
- ☐ Drivers License
- ☐ Known Personally
- ☐ Passport
- ☐ Other:

I.D. Number:

Issued By:

Issued Date:

Expiration Date:

Document Type:

Date/Time Notarized: **AM** **PM**

Document Date:

Fee Charged:

Printed Name and Address of Witness:

Phone Number:

Email:

Witness' Signature:

Comments :

Record Number:

NOTARY RECORD

Printed Name and Address of Signer:

Phone Number:

Email:

Signer's Signature:

Thumb Print:

Service Performed:

- ☐ Oath
- ☐ Acknowledgment
- ☐ Jurat
- ☐ Other:

Identification:

- ☐ I.D Card
- ☐ Credible Witness
- ☐ Drivers License
- ☐ Known Personally
- ☐ Passport
- ☐ Other:

I.D. Number:

Issued By:

Issued Date:

Expiration Date:

Document Type:

Date/Time Notarized: **AM** **PM**

Document Date:

Fee Charged:

Printed Name and Address of Witness:

Phone Number:

Email:

Witness' Signature:

Comments :

Record Number:

NOTARY RECORD

Printed Name and Address of Signer:

Phone Number:

Email:

Signer's Signature:

Thumb Print:

Service Performed:

- ☐ Oath
- ☐ Acknowledgment
- ☐ Jurat
- ☐ Other:

Identification:

- ☐ I.D Card
- ☐ Credible Witness
- ☐ Drivers License
- ☐ Known Personally
- ☐ Passport
- ☐ Other:

I.D. Number:

Issued By:

Issued Date:

Expiration Date:

Document Type:

Date/Time Notarized: **AM** **PM**

Document Date:

Fee Charged:

Printed Name and Address of Witness:

Phone Number:

Email:

Witness' Signature:

Comments :

Record Number:

NOTARY RECORD

Printed Name and Address of Signer:	Phone Number:	Thumb Print:
	Email:	
	Signer's Signature:	

Service Performed:	Identification:		I.D. Number:	
☐ Oath	☐ I.D Card	☐ Credible Witness		
☐ Acknowledgment	☐ Drivers License	☐ Known Personally	Issued By:	
☐ Jurat	☐ Passport			
☐ Other:	☐ Other:		Issued Date:	Expiration Date:
Document Type:	Date/Time Notarized: AM PM		Document Date:	Fee Charged:

Printed Name and Address of Witness:	Phone Number:
	Email:
	Witness' Signature:

Comments :	Record Number:

NOTARY RECORD

Printed Name and Address of Signer:	Phone Number:	Thumb Print:
	Email:	
	Signer's Signature:	

Service Performed:	Identification:		I.D. Number:	
☐ Oath	☐ I.D Card	☐ Credible Witness		
☐ Acknowledgment	☐ Drivers License	☐ Known Personally	Issued By:	
☐ Jurat	☐ Passport			
☐ Other:	☐ Other:		Issued Date:	Expiration Date:
Document Type:	Date/Time Notarized: AM PM		Document Date:	Fee Charged:

Printed Name and Address of Witness:	Phone Number:
	Email:
	Witness' Signature:

Comments :	Record Number:

NOTARY RECORD

Printed Name and Address of Signer:	Phone Number:	Thumb Print:
	Email:	
	Signer's Signature:	

Service Performed:	Identification:		I.D. Number:	
☐ Oath	☐ I.D Card	☐ Credible Witness	Issued By:	
☐ Acknowledgment	☐ Drivers License	☐ Known Personally	Issued Date:	Expiration Date:
☐ Jurat	☐ Passport			
☐ Other:	☐ Other:			
Document Type:	Date/Time Notarized: AM PM		Document Date:	Fee Charged:

Printed Name and Address of Witness:	Phone Number:
	Email:
	Witness' Signature:

Comments :	Record Number:

NOTARY RECORD

Printed Name and Address of Signer:	Phone Number:	Thumb Print:
	Email:	
	Signer's Signature:	

Service Performed:	Identification:		I.D. Number:	
☐ Oath	☐ I.D Card	☐ Credible Witness	Issued By:	
☐ Acknowledgment	☐ Drivers License	☐ Known Personally	Issued Date:	Expiration Date:
☐ Jurat	☐ Passport			
☐ Other:	☐ Other:			
Document Type:	Date/Time Notarized: AM PM		Document Date:	Fee Charged:

Printed Name and Address of Witness:	Phone Number:
	Email:
	Witness' Signature:

Comments :	Record Number:

NOTARY RECORD

Printed Name and Address of Signer:	**Phone Number:**	**Thumb Print:**
	Email:	
	Signer's Signature:	

Service Performed: ☐ Oath ☐ Acknowledgment ☐ Jurat ☐ Other:	**Identification:** ☐ I.D Card ☐ Credible Witness ☐ Drivers License ☐ Known Personally ☐ Passport ☐ Other:	**I.D. Number:**	
		Issued By:	
		Issued Date:	**Expiration Date:**
Document Type:	**Date/Time Notarized:** AM PM	**Document Date:**	**Fee Charged:**

Printed Name and Address of Witness:	**Phone Number:**
	Email:
	Witness' Signature:
Comments :	**Record Number:**

NOTARY RECORD

Printed Name and Address of Signer:	**Phone Number:**	**Thumb Print:**
	Email:	
	Signer's Signature:	

Service Performed: ☐ Oath ☐ Acknowledgment ☐ Jurat ☐ Other:	**Identification:** ☐ I.D Card ☐ Credible Witness ☐ Drivers License ☐ Known Personally ☐ Passport ☐ Other:	**I.D. Number:**	
		Issued By:	
		Issued Date:	**Expiration Date:**
Document Type:	**Date/Time Notarized:** AM PM	**Document Date:**	**Fee Charged:**

Printed Name and Address of Witness:	**Phone Number:**
	Email:
	Witness' Signature:
Comments :	**Record Number:**

NOTARY RECORD

Printed Name and Address of Signer:	Phone Number:	Thumb Print:
	Email:	
	Signer's Signature:	

Service Performed:	Identification:		I.D. Number:	
☐ Oath	☐ I.D Card	☐ Credible Witness	Issued By:	
☐ Acknowledgment	☐ Drivers License	☐ Known Personally		
☐ Jurat	☐ Passport		Issued Date:	Expiration Date:
☐ Other:	☐ Other:			
Document Type:	Date/Time Notarized: AM PM		Document Date:	Fee Charged:

Printed Name and Address of Witness:	Phone Number:
	Email:
	Witness' Signature:

Comments :	Record Number:

NOTARY RECORD

Printed Name and Address of Signer:	Phone Number:	Thumb Print:
	Email:	
	Signer's Signature:	

Service Performed:	Identification:		I.D. Number:	
☐ Oath	☐ I.D Card	☐ Credible Witness	Issued By:	
☐ Acknowledgment	☐ Drivers License	☐ Known Personally		
☐ Jurat	☐ Passport		Issued Date:	Expiration Date:
☐ Other:	☐ Other:			
Document Type:	Date/Time Notarized: AM PM		Document Date:	Fee Charged:

Printed Name and Address of Witness:	Phone Number:
	Email:
	Witness' Signature:

Comments :	Record Number:

NOTARY RECORD

Printed Name and Address of Signer:	**Phone Number:**	**Thumb Print:**
	Email:	
	Signer's Signature:	

Service Performed: ☐ Oath ☐ Acknowledgment ☐ Jurat ☐ Other:	**Identification:** ☐ I.D Card ☐ Credible Witness ☐ Drivers License ☐ Known Personally ☐ Passport ☐ Other:	**I.D. Number:**	
		Issued By:	
		Issued Date:	**Expiration Date:**
Document Type:	**Date/Time Notarized:** AM PM	**Document Date:**	**Fee Charged:**

Printed Name and Address of Witness:	**Phone Number:**
	Email:
	Witness' Signature:
Comments :	**Record Number:**

NOTARY RECORD

Printed Name and Address of Signer:	**Phone Number:**	**Thumb Print:**
	Email:	
	Signer's Signature:	

Service Performed: ☐ Oath ☐ Acknowledgment ☐ Jurat ☐ Other:	**Identification:** ☐ I.D Card ☐ Credible Witness ☐ Drivers License ☐ Known Personally ☐ Passport ☐ Other:	**I.D. Number:**	
		Issued By:	
		Issued Date:	**Expiration Date:**
Document Type:	**Date/Time Notarized:** AM PM	**Document Date:**	**Fee Charged:**

Printed Name and Address of Witness:	**Phone Number:**
	Email:
	Witness' Signature:
Comments :	**Record Number:**

NOTARY RECORD

Printed Name and Address of Signer:	Phone Number:	Thumb Print:
	Email:	
	Signer's Signature:	

Service Performed:	Identification:		I.D. Number:	
☐ Oath	☐ I.D Card	☐ Credible Witness	Issued By:	
☐ Acknowledgment	☐ Drivers License	☐ Known Personally	Issued Date:	Expiration Date:
☐ Jurat	☐ Passport			
☐ Other:	☐ Other:			
Document Type:	Date/Time Notarized: AM PM		Document Date:	Fee Charged:

Printed Name and Address of Witness:	Phone Number:
	Email:
	Witness' Signature:

Comments :	Record Number:

NOTARY RECORD

Printed Name and Address of Signer:	Phone Number:	Thumb Print:
	Email:	
	Signer's Signature:	

Service Performed:	Identification:		I.D. Number:	
☐ Oath	☐ I.D Card	☐ Credible Witness	Issued By:	
☐ Acknowledgment	☐ Drivers License	☐ Known Personally	Issued Date:	Expiration Date:
☐ Jurat	☐ Passport			
☐ Other:	☐ Other:			
Document Type:	Date/Time Notarized: AM PM		Document Date:	Fee Charged:

Printed Name and Address of Witness:	Phone Number:
	Email:
	Witness' Signature:

Comments :	Record Number:

NOTARY RECORD

Printed Name and Address of Signer:	Phone Number:	Thumb Print:
	Email:	
	Signer's Signature:	

Service Performed:	Identification:		I.D. Number:	
☐ Oath	☐ I.D Card	☐ Credible Witness	Issued By:	
☐ Acknowledgment	☐ Drivers License	☐ Known Personally		
☐ Jurat	☐ Passport		Issued Date:	Expiration Date:
☐ Other:	☐ Other:			
Document Type:	Date/Time Notarized: AM PM		Document Date:	Fee Charged:

Printed Name and Address of Witness:	Phone Number:
	Email:
	Witness' Signature:

Comments :	Record Number:

NOTARY RECORD

Printed Name and Address of Signer:	Phone Number:	Thumb Print:
	Email:	
	Signer's Signature:	

Service Performed:	Identification:		I.D. Number:	
☐ Oath	☐ I.D Card	☐ Credible Witness	Issued By:	
☐ Acknowledgment	☐ Drivers License	☐ Known Personally		
☐ Jurat	☐ Passport		Issued Date:	Expiration Date:
☐ Other:	☐ Other:			
Document Type:	Date/Time Notarized: AM PM		Document Date:	Fee Charged:

Printed Name and Address of Witness:	Phone Number:
	Email:
	Witness' Signature:

Comments :	Record Number:

NOTARY RECORD

Printed Name and Address of Signer:	Phone Number:	Thumb Print:
	Email:	
	Signer's Signature:	

Service Performed:	Identification:		I.D. Number:	
☐ Oath	☐ I.D Card	☐ Credible Witness		
☐ Acknowledgment	☐ Drivers License	☐ Known Personally	Issued By:	
☐ Jurat	☐ Passport			
☐ Other:	☐ Other:		Issued Date:	Expiration Date:
Document Type:	Date/Time Notarized: AM PM		Document Date:	Fee Charged:

Printed Name and Address of Witness:	Phone Number:
	Email:
	Witness' Signature:

Comments :	Record Number:

NOTARY RECORD

Printed Name and Address of Signer:	Phone Number:	Thumb Print:
	Email:	
	Signer's Signature:	

Service Performed:	Identification:		I.D. Number:	
☐ Oath	☐ I.D Card	☐ Credible Witness		
☐ Acknowledgment	☐ Drivers License	☐ Known Personally	Issued By:	
☐ Jurat	☐ Passport			
☐ Other:	☐ Other:		Issued Date:	Expiration Date:
Document Type:	Date/Time Notarized: AM PM		Document Date:	Fee Charged:

Printed Name and Address of Witness:	Phone Number:
	Email:
	Witness' Signature:

Comments :	Record Number:

NOTARY RECORD

Printed Name and Address of Signer:	**Phone Number:**	**Thumb Print:**
	Email:	
	Signer's Signature:	

Service Performed: ☐ Oath ☐ Acknowledgment ☐ Jurat ☐ Other:	**Identification:** ☐ I.D Card ☐ Credible Witness ☐ Drivers License ☐ Known Personally ☐ Passport ☐ Other:	**I.D. Number:**	
		Issued By:	
		Issued Date:	**Expiration Date:**
Document Type:	**Date/Time Notarized:** **AM PM**	**Document Date:**	**Fee Charged:**

Printed Name and Address of Witness:	**Phone Number:**
	Email:
	Witness' Signature:
Comments :	**Record Number:**

NOTARY RECORD

Printed Name and Address of Signer:	**Phone Number:**	**Thumb Print:**
	Email:	
	Signer's Signature:	

Service Performed: ☐ Oath ☐ Acknowledgment ☐ Jurat ☐ Other:	**Identification:** ☐ I.D Card ☐ Credible Witness ☐ Drivers License ☐ Known Personally ☐ Passport ☐ Other:	**I.D. Number:**	
		Issued By:	
		Issued Date:	**Expiration Date:**
Document Type:	**Date/Time Notarized:** **AM PM**	**Document Date:**	**Fee Charged:**

Printed Name and Address of Witness:	**Phone Number:**
	Email:
	Witness' Signature:
Comments :	**Record Number:**

NOTARY RECORD

Printed Name and Address of Signer:	Phone Number:	Thumb Print:
	Email:	
	Signer's Signature:	

Service Performed:	Identification:		I.D. Number:	
☐ Oath	☐ I.D Card	☐ Credible Witness	Issued By:	
☐ Acknowledgment	☐ Drivers License	☐ Known Personally		
☐ Jurat	☐ Passport		Issued Date:	Expiration Date:
☐ Other:	☐ Other:			
Document Type:	Date/Time Notarized: AM PM		Document Date:	Fee Charged:

Printed Name and Address of Witness:	Phone Number:
	Email:
	Witness' Signature:

Comments :	Record Number:

NOTARY RECORD

Printed Name and Address of Signer:	Phone Number:	Thumb Print:
	Email:	
	Signer's Signature:	

Service Performed:	Identification:		I.D. Number:	
☐ Oath	☐ I.D Card	☐ Credible Witness	Issued By:	
☐ Acknowledgment	☐ Drivers License	☐ Known Personally		
☐ Jurat	☐ Passport		Issued Date:	Expiration Date:
☐ Other:	☐ Other:			
Document Type:	Date/Time Notarized: AM PM		Document Date:	Fee Charged:

Printed Name and Address of Witness:	Phone Number:
	Email:
	Witness' Signature:

Comments :	Record Number:

NOTARY RECORD

Printed Name and Address of Signer:	Phone Number:	Thumb Print:
	Email:	
	Signer's Signature:	

Service Performed:	Identification:		I.D. Number:	
☐ Oath	☐ I.D Card	☐ Credible Witness		
☐ Acknowledgment	☐ Drivers License	☐ Known Personally	Issued By:	
☐ Jurat	☐ Passport			
☐ Other:	☐ Other:		Issued Date:	Expiration Date:
Document Type:	Date/Time Notarized:	AM PM	Document Date:	Fee Charged:

Printed Name and Address of Witness:	Phone Number:
	Email:
	Witness' Signature:

Comments :	Record Number:

NOTARY RECORD

Printed Name and Address of Signer:	Phone Number:	Thumb Print:
	Email:	
	Signer's Signature:	

Service Performed:	Identification:		I.D. Number:	
☐ Oath	☐ I.D Card	☐ Credible Witness		
☐ Acknowledgment	☐ Drivers License	☐ Known Personally	Issued By:	
☐ Jurat	☐ Passport			
☐ Other:	☐ Other:		Issued Date:	Expiration Date:
Document Type:	Date/Time Notarized:	AM PM	Document Date:	Fee Charged:

Printed Name and Address of Witness:	Phone Number:
	Email:
	Witness' Signature:

Comments :	Record Number:

NOTARY RECORD

Printed Name and Address of Signer:	Phone Number:	Thumb Print:
	Email:	
	Signer's Signature:	

Service Performed:	Identification:		I.D. Number:	
☐ Oath	☐ I.D Card	☐ Credible Witness	Issued By:	
☐ Acknowledgment	☐ Drivers License	☐ Known Personally		
☐ Jurat	☐ Passport		Issued Date:	Expiration Date:
☐ Other:	☐ Other:			
Document Type:	Date/Time Notarized: AM PM		Document Date:	Fee Charged:

Printed Name and Address of Witness:	Phone Number:
	Email:
	Witness' Signature:

Comments :	Record Number:

NOTARY RECORD

Printed Name and Address of Signer:	Phone Number:	Thumb Print:
	Email:	
	Signer's Signature:	

Service Performed:	Identification:		I.D. Number:	
☐ Oath	☐ I.D Card	☐ Credible Witness	Issued By:	
☐ Acknowledgment	☐ Drivers License	☐ Known Personally		
☐ Jurat	☐ Passport		Issued Date:	Expiration Date:
☐ Other:	☐ Other:			
Document Type:	Date/Time Notarized: AM PM		Document Date:	Fee Charged:

Printed Name and Address of Witness:	Phone Number:
	Email:
	Witness' Signature:

Comments :	Record Number:

NOTARY RECORD

Printed Name and Address of Signer:	**Phone Number:**	**Thumb Print:**
	Email:	
	Signer's Signature:	

Service Performed: ☐ Oath ☐ Acknowledgment ☐ Jurat ☐ Other:	**Identification:** ☐ I.D Card ☐ Credible Witness ☐ Drivers License ☐ Known Personally ☐ Passport ☐ Other:	**I.D. Number:**	
		Issued By:	
		Issued Date:	**Expiration Date:**
Document Type:	**Date/Time Notarized:** AM PM	**Document Date:**	**Fee Charged:**

Printed Name and Address of Witness:	**Phone Number:**
	Email:
	Witness' Signature:
Comments :	**Record Number:**

NOTARY RECORD

Printed Name and Address of Signer:	**Phone Number:**	**Thumb Print:**
	Email:	
	Signer's Signature:	

Service Performed: ☐ Oath ☐ Acknowledgment ☐ Jurat ☐ Other:	**Identification:** ☐ I.D Card ☐ Credible Witness ☐ Drivers License ☐ Known Personally ☐ Passport ☐ Other:	**I.D. Number:**	
		Issued By:	
		Issued Date:	**Expiration Date:**
Document Type:	**Date/Time Notarized:** AM PM	**Document Date:**	**Fee Charged:**

Printed Name and Address of Witness:	**Phone Number:**
	Email:
	Witness' Signature:
Comments :	**Record Number:**

NOTARY RECORD

Printed Name and Address of Signer:	Phone Number:	Thumb Print:
	Email:	
	Signer's Signature:	

Service Performed:	Identification:		I.D. Number:	
☐ Oath	☐ I.D Card	☐ Credible Witness		
☐ Acknowledgment	☐ Drivers License	☐ Known Personally	Issued By:	
☐ Jurat	☐ Passport			
☐ Other:	☐ Other:		Issued Date:	Expiration Date:
Document Type:	Date/Time Notarized: AM PM		Document Date:	Fee Charged:

Printed Name and Address of Witness:	Phone Number:
	Email:
	Witness' Signature:

Comments :	Record Number:

NOTARY RECORD

Printed Name and Address of Signer:	Phone Number:	Thumb Print:
	Email:	
	Signer's Signature:	

Service Performed:	Identification:		I.D. Number:	
☐ Oath	☐ I.D Card	☐ Credible Witness		
☐ Acknowledgment	☐ Drivers License	☐ Known Personally	Issued By:	
☐ Jurat	☐ Passport			
☐ Other:	☐ Other:		Issued Date:	Expiration Date:
Document Type:	Date/Time Notarized: AM PM		Document Date:	Fee Charged:

Printed Name and Address of Witness:	Phone Number:
	Email:
	Witness' Signature:

Comments :	Record Number:

NOTARY RECORD

Printed Name and Address of Signer:

Phone Number:

Email:

Signer's Signature:

Thumb Print:

Service Performed:
- ☐ Oath
- ☐ Acknowledgment
- ☐ Jurat
- ☐ Other:

Identification:
- ☐ I.D Card
- ☐ Credible Witness
- ☐ Drivers License
- ☐ Known Personally
- ☐ Passport
- ☐ Other:

I.D. Number:

Issued By:

Issued Date:

Expiration Date:

Document Type:

Date/Time Notarized: **AM** **PM**

Document Date:

Fee Charged:

Printed Name and Address of Witness:

Phone Number:

Email:

Witness' Signature:

Comments :

Record Number:

NOTARY RECORD

Printed Name and Address of Signer:

Phone Number:

Email:

Signer's Signature:

Thumb Print:

Service Performed:
- ☐ Oath
- ☐ Acknowledgment
- ☐ Jurat
- ☐ Other:

Identification:
- ☐ I.D Card
- ☐ Credible Witness
- ☐ Drivers License
- ☐ Known Personally
- ☐ Passport
- ☐ Other:

I.D. Number:

Issued By:

Issued Date:

Expiration Date:

Document Type:

Date/Time Notarized: **AM** **PM**

Document Date:

Fee Charged:

Printed Name and Address of Witness:

Phone Number:

Email:

Witness' Signature:

Comments :

Record Number:

NOTARY RECORD

Printed Name and Address of Signer:	Phone Number:	Thumb Print:
	Email:	
	Signer's Signature:	

Service Performed:	Identification:		I.D. Number:	
☐ Oath	☐ I.D Card	☐ Credible Witness	Issued By:	
☐ Acknowledgment	☐ Drivers License	☐ Known Personally	Issued Date:	Expiration Date:
☐ Jurat	☐ Passport			
☐ Other:	☐ Other:			
Document Type:	Date/Time Notarized: AM PM		Document Date:	Fee Charged:

Printed Name and Address of Witness:	Phone Number:
	Email:
	Witness' Signature:

Comments :	Record Number:

NOTARY RECORD

Printed Name and Address of Signer:	Phone Number:	Thumb Print:
	Email:	
	Signer's Signature:	

Service Performed:	Identification:		I.D. Number:	
☐ Oath	☐ I.D Card	☐ Credible Witness	Issued By:	
☐ Acknowledgment	☐ Drivers License	☐ Known Personally	Issued Date:	Expiration Date:
☐ Jurat	☐ Passport			
☐ Other:	☐ Other:			
Document Type:	Date/Time Notarized: AM PM		Document Date:	Fee Charged:

Printed Name and Address of Witness:	Phone Number:
	Email:
	Witness' Signature:

Comments :	Record Number:

NOTARY RECORD

Printed Name and Address of Signer:	Phone Number:	Thumb Print:
	Email:	
	Signer's Signature:	

Service Performed:	Identification:		I.D. Number:	
☐ Oath	☐ I.D Card	☐ Credible Witness		
☐ Acknowledgment	☐ Drivers License	☐ Known Personally	Issued By:	
☐ Jurat	☐ Passport			
☐ Other:	☐ Other:		Issued Date:	Expiration Date:
Document Type:	Date/Time Notarized: AM PM		Document Date:	Fee Charged:

Printed Name and Address of Witness:	Phone Number:
	Email:
	Witness' Signature:

Comments :	Record Number:

NOTARY RECORD

Printed Name and Address of Signer:	Phone Number:	Thumb Print:
	Email:	
	Signer's Signature:	

Service Performed:	Identification:		I.D. Number:	
☐ Oath	☐ I.D Card	☐ Credible Witness		
☐ Acknowledgment	☐ Drivers License	☐ Known Personally	Issued By:	
☐ Jurat	☐ Passport			
☐ Other:	☐ Other:		Issued Date:	Expiration Date:
Document Type:	Date/Time Notarized: AM PM		Document Date:	Fee Charged:

Printed Name and Address of Witness:	Phone Number:
	Email:
	Witness' Signature:

Comments :	Record Number:

NOTARY RECORD

Printed Name and Address of Signer:

Phone Number:

Email:

Signer's Signature:

Thumb Print:

Service Performed:

- ☐ Oath
- ☐ Acknowledgment
- ☐ Jurat
- ☐ Other:

Identification:

- ☐ I.D Card
- ☐ Credible Witness
- ☐ Drivers License
- ☐ Known Personally
- ☐ Passport
- ☐ Other:

I.D. Number:

Issued By:

Issued Date:

Expiration Date:

Document Type:

Date/Time Notarized: **AM** **PM**

Document Date:

Fee Charged:

Printed Name and Address of Witness:

Phone Number:

Email:

Witness' Signature:

Comments :

Record Number:

NOTARY RECORD

Printed Name and Address of Signer:

Phone Number:

Email:

Signer's Signature:

Thumb Print:

Service Performed:

- ☐ Oath
- ☐ Acknowledgment
- ☐ Jurat
- ☐ Other:

Identification:

- ☐ I.D Card
- ☐ Credible Witness
- ☐ Drivers License
- ☐ Known Personally
- ☐ Passport
- ☐ Other:

I.D. Number:

Issued By:

Issued Date:

Expiration Date:

Document Type:

Date/Time Notarized: **AM** **PM**

Document Date:

Fee Charged:

Printed Name and Address of Witness:

Phone Number:

Email:

Witness' Signature:

Comments :

Record Number:

NOTARY RECORD

Printed Name and Address of Signer:

Phone Number:

Email:

Signer's Signature:

Thumb Print:

Service Performed:
- ☐ Oath
- ☐ Acknowledgment
- ☐ Jurat
- ☐ Other:

Identification:
- ☐ I.D Card
- ☐ Credible Witness
- ☐ Drivers License
- ☐ Known Personally
- ☐ Passport
- ☐ Other:

I.D. Number:

Issued By:

Issued Date:

Expiration Date:

Document Type:

Date/Time Notarized: **AM** **PM**

Document Date:

Fee Charged:

Printed Name and Address of Witness:

Phone Number:

Email:

Witness' Signature:

Comments :

Record Number:

NOTARY RECORD

Printed Name and Address of Signer:

Phone Number:

Email:

Signer's Signature:

Thumb Print:

Service Performed:
- ☐ Oath
- ☐ Acknowledgment
- ☐ Jurat
- ☐ Other:

Identification:
- ☐ I.D Card
- ☐ Credible Witness
- ☐ Drivers License
- ☐ Known Personally
- ☐ Passport
- ☐ Other:

I.D. Number:

Issued By:

Issued Date:

Expiration Date:

Document Type:

Date/Time Notarized: **AM** **PM**

Document Date:

Fee Charged:

Printed Name and Address of Witness:

Phone Number:

Email:

Witness' Signature:

Comments :

Record Number:

NOTARY RECORD

Printed Name and Address of Signer:	**Phone Number:**	**Thumb Print:**
	Email:	
	Signer's Signature:	

Service Performed: ☐ Oath ☐ Acknowledgment ☐ Jurat ☐ Other:	**Identification:** ☐ I.D Card ☐ Credible Witness ☐ Drivers License ☐ Known Personally ☐ Passport ☐ Other:	**I.D. Number:**	
		Issued By:	
		Issued Date:	**Expiration Date:**
Document Type:	**Date/Time Notarized:** AM PM	**Document Date:**	**Fee Charged:**

Printed Name and Address of Witness:	**Phone Number:**
	Email:
	Witness' Signature:

Comments :	**Record Number:**

NOTARY RECORD

Printed Name and Address of Signer:	**Phone Number:**	**Thumb Print:**
	Email:	
	Signer's Signature:	

Service Performed: ☐ Oath ☐ Acknowledgment ☐ Jurat ☐ Other:	**Identification:** ☐ I.D Card ☐ Credible Witness ☐ Drivers License ☐ Known Personally ☐ Passport ☐ Other:	**I.D. Number:**	
		Issued By:	
		Issued Date:	**Expiration Date:**
Document Type:	**Date/Time Notarized:** AM PM	**Document Date:**	**Fee Charged:**

Printed Name and Address of Witness:	**Phone Number:**
	Email:
	Witness' Signature:

Comments :	**Record Number:**

NOTARY RECORD

Printed Name and Address of Signer:	Phone Number:	Thumb Print:
	Email:	
	Signer's Signature:	

Service Performed:	Identification:		I.D. Number:	
☐ Oath	☐ I.D Card	☐ Credible Witness	Issued By:	
☐ Acknowledgment	☐ Drivers License	☐ Known Personally		
☐ Jurat	☐ Passport		Issued Date:	Expiration Date:
☐ Other:	☐ Other:			
Document Type:	Date/Time Notarized:	AM PM	Document Date:	Fee Charged:

Printed Name and Address of Witness:	Phone Number:
	Email:
	Witness' Signature:

Comments :	Record Number:

NOTARY RECORD

Printed Name and Address of Signer:	Phone Number:	Thumb Print:
	Email:	
	Signer's Signature:	

Service Performed:	Identification:		I.D. Number:	
☐ Oath	☐ I.D Card	☐ Credible Witness	Issued By:	
☐ Acknowledgment	☐ Drivers License	☐ Known Personally		
☐ Jurat	☐ Passport		Issued Date:	Expiration Date:
☐ Other:	☐ Other:			
Document Type:	Date/Time Notarized:	AM PM	Document Date:	Fee Charged:

Printed Name and Address of Witness:	Phone Number:
	Email:
	Witness' Signature:

Comments :	Record Number:

NOTARY RECORD

Printed Name and Address of Signer:

Phone Number:

Email:

Signer's Signature:

Thumb Print:

Service Performed:

- ☐ Oath
- ☐ Acknowledgment
- ☐ Jurat
- ☐ Other:

Identification:

- ☐ I.D Card
- ☐ Credible Witness
- ☐ Drivers License
- ☐ Known Personally
- ☐ Passport
- ☐ Other:

I.D. Number:

Issued By:

Issued Date:

Expiration Date:

Document Type:

Date/Time Notarized: AM PM

Document Date:

Fee Charged:

Printed Name and Address of Witness:

Phone Number:

Email:

Witness' Signature:

Comments :

Record Number:

NOTARY RECORD

Printed Name and Address of Signer:

Phone Number:

Email:

Signer's Signature:

Thumb Print:

Service Performed:

- ☐ Oath
- ☐ Acknowledgment
- ☐ Jurat
- ☐ Other:

Identification:

- ☐ I.D Card
- ☐ Credible Witness
- ☐ Drivers License
- ☐ Known Personally
- ☐ Passport
- ☐ Other:

I.D. Number:

Issued By:

Issued Date:

Expiration Date:

Document Type:

Date/Time Notarized: AM PM

Document Date:

Fee Charged:

Printed Name and Address of Witness:

Phone Number:

Email:

Witness' Signature:

Comments :

Record Number:

NOTARY RECORD

Printed Name and Address of Signer:	**Phone Number:**	**Thumb Print:**
	Email:	
	Signer's Signature:	

Service Performed: ☐ Oath ☐ Acknowledgment ☐ Jurat ☐ Other:	**Identification:** ☐ I.D Card ☐ Credible Witness ☐ Drivers License ☐ Known Personally ☐ Passport ☐ Other:	**I.D. Number:**	
		Issued By:	
		Issued Date:	**Expiration Date:**
Document Type:	**Date/Time Notarized:** AM PM	**Document Date:**	**Fee Charged:**

Printed Name and Address of Witness:	**Phone Number:**
	Email:
	Witness' Signature:
Comments :	**Record Number:**

NOTARY RECORD

Printed Name and Address of Signer:	**Phone Number:**	**Thumb Print:**
	Email:	
	Signer's Signature:	

Service Performed: ☐ Oath ☐ Acknowledgment ☐ Jurat ☐ Other:	**Identification:** ☐ I.D Card ☐ Credible Witness ☐ Drivers License ☐ Known Personally ☐ Passport ☐ Other:	**I.D. Number:**	
		Issued By:	
		Issued Date:	**Expiration Date:**
Document Type:	**Date/Time Notarized:** AM PM	**Document Date:**	**Fee Charged:**

Printed Name and Address of Witness:	**Phone Number:**
	Email:
	Witness' Signature:
Comments :	**Record Number:**

NOTARY RECORD

Printed Name and Address of Signer:	Phone Number:	Thumb Print:
	Email:	
	Signer's Signature:	

Service Performed:	Identification:		I.D. Number:	
☐ Oath	☐ I.D Card	☐ Credible Witness	Issued By:	
☐ Acknowledgment	☐ Drivers License	☐ Known Personally		
☐ Jurat	☐ Passport		Issued Date:	Expiration Date:
☐ Other:	☐ Other:			
Document Type:	Date/Time Notarized: AM PM		Document Date:	Fee Charged:

Printed Name and Address of Witness:	Phone Number:
	Email:
	Witness' Signature:

Comments :	Record Number:

NOTARY RECORD

Printed Name and Address of Signer:	Phone Number:	Thumb Print:
	Email:	
	Signer's Signature:	

Service Performed:	Identification:		I.D. Number:	
☐ Oath	☐ I.D Card	☐ Credible Witness	Issued By:	
☐ Acknowledgment	☐ Drivers License	☐ Known Personally		
☐ Jurat	☐ Passport		Issued Date:	Expiration Date:
☐ Other:	☐ Other:			
Document Type:	Date/Time Notarized: AM PM		Document Date:	Fee Charged:

Printed Name and Address of Witness:	Phone Number:
	Email:
	Witness' Signature:

Comments :	Record Number:

NOTARY RECORD

Printed Name and Address of Signer:	Phone Number:	Thumb Print:
	Email:	
	Signer's Signature:	

Service Performed:	Identification:		I.D. Number:	
☐ Oath	☐ I.D Card	☐ Credible Witness	Issued By:	
☐ Acknowledgment	☐ Drivers License	☐ Known Personally	Issued Date:	Expiration Date:
☐ Jurat	☐ Passport			
☐ Other:	☐ Other:			
Document Type:	Date/Time Notarized: AM PM		Document Date:	Fee Charged:

Printed Name and Address of Witness:	Phone Number:
	Email:
	Witness' Signature:

Comments :	Record Number:

NOTARY RECORD

Printed Name and Address of Signer:	Phone Number:	Thumb Print:
	Email:	
	Signer's Signature:	

Service Performed:	Identification:		I.D. Number:	
☐ Oath	☐ I.D Card	☐ Credible Witness	Issued By:	
☐ Acknowledgment	☐ Drivers License	☐ Known Personally	Issued Date:	Expiration Date:
☐ Jurat	☐ Passport			
☐ Other:	☐ Other:			
Document Type:	Date/Time Notarized: AM PM		Document Date:	Fee Charged:

Printed Name and Address of Witness:	Phone Number:
	Email:
	Witness' Signature:

Comments :	Record Number:

NOTARY RECORD

Printed Name and Address of Signer:	Phone Number:	Thumb Print:
	Email:	
	Signer's Signature:	

Service Performed:	Identification:	I.D. Number:	
☐ Oath ☐ Acknowledgment ☐ Jurat ☐ Other:	☐ I.D Card ☐ Credible Witness ☐ Drivers License ☐ Known Personally ☐ Passport ☐ Other:	Issued By:	
		Issued Date:	Expiration Date:
Document Type:	Date/Time Notarized: AM PM	Document Date:	Fee Charged:

Printed Name and Address of Witness:	Phone Number:
	Email:
	Witness' Signature:

Comments :	Record Number:

NOTARY RECORD

Printed Name and Address of Signer:	Phone Number:	Thumb Print:
	Email:	
	Signer's Signature:	

Service Performed:	Identification:	I.D. Number:	
☐ Oath ☐ Acknowledgment ☐ Jurat ☐ Other:	☐ I.D Card ☐ Credible Witness ☐ Drivers License ☐ Known Personally ☐ Passport ☐ Other:	Issued By:	
		Issued Date:	Expiration Date:
Document Type:	Date/Time Notarized: AM PM	Document Date:	Fee Charged:

Printed Name and Address of Witness:	Phone Number:
	Email:
	Witness' Signature:

Comments :	Record Number:

NOTARY RECORD

Printed Name and Address of Signer:	Phone Number:	Thumb Print:
	Email:	
	Signer's Signature:	

Service Performed:	Identification:		I.D. Number:	
☐ Oath	☐ I.D Card	☐ Credible Witness	Issued By:	
☐ Acknowledgment	☐ Drivers License	☐ Known Personally		
☐ Jurat	☐ Passport		Issued Date:	Expiration Date:
☐ Other:	☐ Other:			
Document Type:	Date/Time Notarized:	AM PM	Document Date:	Fee Charged:

Printed Name and Address of Witness:	Phone Number:
	Email:
	Witness' Signature:

Comments :	Record Number:

NOTARY RECORD

Printed Name and Address of Signer:	Phone Number:	Thumb Print:
	Email:	
	Signer's Signature:	

Service Performed:	Identification:		I.D. Number:	
☐ Oath	☐ I.D Card	☐ Credible Witness	Issued By:	
☐ Acknowledgment	☐ Drivers License	☐ Known Personally		
☐ Jurat	☐ Passport		Issued Date:	Expiration Date:
☐ Other:	☐ Other:			
Document Type:	Date/Time Notarized:	AM PM	Document Date:	Fee Charged:

Printed Name and Address of Witness:	Phone Number:
	Email:
	Witness' Signature:

Comments :	Record Number:

NOTARY RECORD

Printed Name and Address of Signer:	Phone Number:	Thumb Print:
	Email:	
	Signer's Signature:	

Service Performed:	Identification:		I.D. Number:	
☐ Oath	☐ I.D Card	☐ Credible Witness		
☐ Acknowledgment	☐ Drivers License	☐ Known Personally	Issued By:	
☐ Jurat	☐ Passport			
☐ Other:	☐ Other:		Issued Date:	Expiration Date:
Document Type:	Date/Time Notarized: AM PM		Document Date:	Fee Charged:

Printed Name and Address of Witness:	Phone Number:
	Email:
	Witness' Signature:

Comments :	Record Number:

NOTARY RECORD

Printed Name and Address of Signer:	Phone Number:	Thumb Print:
	Email:	
	Signer's Signature:	

Service Performed:	Identification:		I.D. Number:	
☐ Oath	☐ I.D Card	☐ Credible Witness		
☐ Acknowledgment	☐ Drivers License	☐ Known Personally	Issued By:	
☐ Jurat	☐ Passport			
☐ Other:	☐ Other:		Issued Date:	Expiration Date:
Document Type:	Date/Time Notarized: AM PM		Document Date:	Fee Charged:

Printed Name and Address of Witness:	Phone Number:
	Email:
	Witness' Signature:

Comments :	Record Number:

NOTARY RECORD

Printed Name and Address of Signer:	**Phone Number:**	**Thumb Print:**
	Email:	
	Signer's Signature:	

Service Performed:	**Identification:**		**I.D. Number:**	
☐ Oath	☐ I.D Card	☐ Credible Witness		
☐ Acknowledgment	☐ Drivers License	☐ Known Personally	**Issued By:**	
☐ Jurat	☐ Passport			
☐ Other:	☐ Other:		**Issued Date:**	**Expiration Date:**
Document Type:	**Date/Time Notarized:** AM PM		**Document Date:**	**Fee Charged:**

Printed Name and Address of Witness:	**Phone Number:**
	Email:
	Witness' Signature:

Comments :	**Record Number:**

NOTARY RECORD

Printed Name and Address of Signer:	**Phone Number:**	**Thumb Print:**
	Email:	
	Signer's Signature:	

Service Performed:	**Identification:**		**I.D. Number:**	
☐ Oath	☐ I.D Card	☐ Credible Witness		
☐ Acknowledgment	☐ Drivers License	☐ Known Personally	**Issued By:**	
☐ Jurat	☐ Passport			
☐ Other:	☐ Other:		**Issued Date:**	**Expiration Date:**
Document Type:	**Date/Time Notarized:** AM PM		**Document Date:**	**Fee Charged:**

Printed Name and Address of Witness:	**Phone Number:**
	Email:
	Witness' Signature:

Comments :	**Record Number:**

NOTARY RECORD

Printed Name and Address of Signer:	**Phone Number:**	**Thumb Print:**
	Email:	
	Signer's Signature:	

Service Performed: ☐ Oath ☐ Acknowledgment ☐ Jurat ☐ Other:	**Identification:** ☐ I.D Card ☐ Credible Witness ☐ Drivers License ☐ Known Personally ☐ Passport ☐ Other:	**I.D. Number:**	
		Issued By:	
		Issued Date:	**Expiration Date:**
Document Type:	**Date/Time Notarized:** **AM PM**	**Document Date:**	**Fee Charged:**

Printed Name and Address of Witness:	**Phone Number:**
	Email:
	Witness' Signature:
Comments :	**Record Number:**

NOTARY RECORD

Printed Name and Address of Signer:	**Phone Number:**	**Thumb Print:**
	Email:	
	Signer's Signature:	

Service Performed: ☐ Oath ☐ Acknowledgment ☐ Jurat ☐ Other:	**Identification:** ☐ I.D Card ☐ Credible Witness ☐ Drivers License ☐ Known Personally ☐ Passport ☐ Other:	**I.D. Number:**	
		Issued By:	
		Issued Date:	**Expiration Date:**
Document Type:	**Date/Time Notarized:** **AM PM**	**Document Date:**	**Fee Charged:**

Printed Name and Address of Witness:	**Phone Number:**
	Email:
	Witness' Signature:
Comments :	**Record Number:**

NOTARY RECORD

Printed Name and Address of Signer:

Phone Number:

Email:

Signer's Signature:

Thumb Print:

Service Performed:

- ☐ Oath
- ☐ Acknowledgment
- ☐ Jurat
- ☐ Other:

Identification:

- ☐ I.D Card
- ☐ Credible Witness
- ☐ Drivers License
- ☐ Known Personally
- ☐ Passport
- ☐ Other:

I.D. Number:

Issued By:

Issued Date:

Expiration Date:

Document Type:

Date/Time Notarized: **AM PM**

Document Date:

Fee Charged:

Printed Name and Address of Witness:

Phone Number:

Email:

Witness' Signature:

Comments :

Record Number:

NOTARY RECORD

Printed Name and Address of Signer:

Phone Number:

Email:

Signer's Signature:

Thumb Print:

Service Performed:

- ☐ Oath
- ☐ Acknowledgment
- ☐ Jurat
- ☐ Other:

Identification:

- ☐ I.D Card
- ☐ Credible Witness
- ☐ Drivers License
- ☐ Known Personally
- ☐ Passport
- ☐ Other:

I.D. Number:

Issued By:

Issued Date:

Expiration Date:

Document Type:

Date/Time Notarized: **AM PM**

Document Date:

Fee Charged:

Printed Name and Address of Witness:

Phone Number:

Email:

Witness' Signature:

Comments :

Record Number:

NOTARY RECORD

Printed Name and Address of Signer:	**Phone Number:**	**Thumb Print:**
	Email:	
	Signer's Signature:	

Service Performed: ☐ Oath ☐ Acknowledgment ☐ Jurat ☐ Other:	**Identification:** ☐ I.D Card ☐ Credible Witness ☐ Drivers License ☐ Known Personally ☐ Passport ☐ Other:	**I.D. Number:**	
		Issued By:	
		Issued Date:	**Expiration Date:**
Document Type:	**Date/Time Notarized:** AM PM	**Document Date:**	**Fee Charged:**

Printed Name and Address of Witness:	**Phone Number:**
	Email:
	Witness' Signature:
Comments :	**Record Number:**

NOTARY RECORD

Printed Name and Address of Signer:	**Phone Number:**	**Thumb Print:**
	Email:	
	Signer's Signature:	

Service Performed: ☐ Oath ☐ Acknowledgment ☐ Jurat ☐ Other:	**Identification:** ☐ I.D Card ☐ Credible Witness ☐ Drivers License ☐ Known Personally ☐ Passport ☐ Other:	**I.D. Number:**	
		Issued By:	
		Issued Date:	**Expiration Date:**
Document Type:	**Date/Time Notarized:** AM PM	**Document Date:**	**Fee Charged:**

Printed Name and Address of Witness:	**Phone Number:**
	Email:
	Witness' Signature:
Comments :	**Record Number:**

NOTARY RECORD

Printed Name and Address of Signer:	Phone Number:	Thumb Print:
	Email:	
	Signer's Signature:	

Service Performed:	Identification:		I.D. Number:	
☐ Oath	☐ I.D Card	☐ Credible Witness	Issued By:	
☐ Acknowledgment	☐ Drivers License	☐ Known Personally	Issued Date:	Expiration Date:
☐ Jurat	☐ Passport			
☐ Other:	☐ Other:			
Document Type:	Date/Time Notarized: AM PM		Document Date:	Fee Charged:

Printed Name and Address of Witness:	Phone Number:
	Email:
	Witness' Signature:

Comments :	Record Number:

NOTARY RECORD

Printed Name and Address of Signer:	Phone Number:	Thumb Print:
	Email:	
	Signer's Signature:	

Service Performed:	Identification:		I.D. Number:	
☐ Oath	☐ I.D Card	☐ Credible Witness	Issued By:	
☐ Acknowledgment	☐ Drivers License	☐ Known Personally	Issued Date:	Expiration Date:
☐ Jurat	☐ Passport			
☐ Other:	☐ Other:			
Document Type:	Date/Time Notarized: AM PM		Document Date:	Fee Charged:

Printed Name and Address of Witness:	Phone Number:
	Email:
	Witness' Signature:

Comments :	Record Number:

NOTARY RECORD

Printed Name and Address of Signer:	**Phone Number:**	**Thumb Print:**
	Email:	
	Signer's Signature:	

Service Performed: ☐ Oath ☐ Acknowledgment ☐ Jurat ☐ Other:	**Identification:** ☐ I.D Card ☐ Credible Witness ☐ Drivers License ☐ Known Personally ☐ Passport ☐ Other:	**I.D. Number:**	
		Issued By:	
		Issued Date:	**Expiration Date:**
Document Type:	**Date/Time Notarized:** AM PM	**Document Date:**	**Fee Charged:**

Printed Name and Address of Witness:	**Phone Number:**
	Email:
	Witness' Signature:
Comments :	**Record Number:**

NOTARY RECORD

Printed Name and Address of Signer:	**Phone Number:**	**Thumb Print:**
	Email:	
	Signer's Signature:	

Service Performed: ☐ Oath ☐ Acknowledgment ☐ Jurat ☐ Other:	**Identification:** ☐ I.D Card ☐ Credible Witness ☐ Drivers License ☐ Known Personally ☐ Passport ☐ Other:	**I.D. Number:**	
		Issued By:	
		Issued Date:	**Expiration Date:**
Document Type:	**Date/Time Notarized:** AM PM	**Document Date:**	**Fee Charged:**

Printed Name and Address of Witness:	**Phone Number:**
	Email:
	Witness' Signature:
Comments :	**Record Number:**

NOTARY RECORD

Printed Name and Address of Signer:	**Phone Number:**	**Thumb Print:**
	Email:	
	Signer's Signature:	

Service Performed: ☐ Oath ☐ Acknowledgment ☐ Jurat ☐ Other:	**Identification:** ☐ I.D Card ☐ Credible Witness ☐ Drivers License ☐ Known Personally ☐ Passport ☐ Other:	**I.D. Number:**	
		Issued By:	
		Issued Date:	**Expiration Date:**
Document Type:	**Date/Time Notarized:** **AM** **PM**	**Document Date:**	**Fee Charged:**

Printed Name and Address of Witness:	**Phone Number:**
	Email:
	Witness' Signature:
Comments :	**Record Number:**

NOTARY RECORD

Printed Name and Address of Signer:	**Phone Number:**	**Thumb Print:**
	Email:	
	Signer's Signature:	

Service Performed: ☐ Oath ☐ Acknowledgment ☐ Jurat ☐ Other:	**Identification:** ☐ I.D Card ☐ Credible Witness ☐ Drivers License ☐ Known Personally ☐ Passport ☐ Other:	**I.D. Number:**	
		Issued By:	
		Issued Date:	**Expiration Date:**
Document Type:	**Date/Time Notarized:** **AM** **PM**	**Document Date:**	**Fee Charged:**

Printed Name and Address of Witness:	**Phone Number:**
	Email:
	Witness' Signature:
Comments :	**Record Number:**

NOTARY RECORD

Printed Name and Address of Signer:	**Phone Number:**	**Thumb Print:**
	Email:	
	Signer's Signature:	

Service Performed: ☐ Oath ☐ Acknowledgment ☐ Jurat ☐ Other:	**Identification:** ☐ I.D Card ☐ Credible Witness ☐ Drivers License ☐ Known Personally ☐ Passport ☐ Other:	**I.D. Number:**	
		Issued By:	
		Issued Date:	**Expiration Date:**
Document Type:	**Date/Time Notarized:** AM PM	**Document Date:**	**Fee Charged:**

Printed Name and Address of Witness:	**Phone Number:**
	Email:
	Witness' Signature:

Comments :	**Record Number:**

NOTARY RECORD

Printed Name and Address of Signer:	**Phone Number:**	**Thumb Print:**
	Email:	
	Signer's Signature:	

Service Performed: ☐ Oath ☐ Acknowledgment ☐ Jurat ☐ Other:	**Identification:** ☐ I.D Card ☐ Credible Witness ☐ Drivers License ☐ Known Personally ☐ Passport ☐ Other:	**I.D. Number:**	
		Issued By:	
		Issued Date:	**Expiration Date:**
Document Type:	**Date/Time Notarized:** AM PM	**Document Date:**	**Fee Charged:**

Printed Name and Address of Witness:	**Phone Number:**
	Email:
	Witness' Signature:

Comments :	**Record Number:**

NOTARY RECORD

Printed Name and Address of Signer:	Phone Number:	Thumb Print:
	Email:	
	Signer's Signature:	

Service Performed:	Identification:		I.D. Number:	
☐ Oath	☐ I.D Card	☐ Credible Witness		
☐ Acknowledgment	☐ Drivers License	☐ Known Personally	Issued By:	
☐ Jurat	☐ Passport			
☐ Other:	☐ Other:		Issued Date:	Expiration Date:
Document Type:	Date/Time Notarized:	AM PM	Document Date:	Fee Charged:

Printed Name and Address of Witness:	Phone Number:
	Email:
	Witness' Signature:

Comments :	Record Number:

NOTARY RECORD

Printed Name and Address of Signer:	Phone Number:	Thumb Print:
	Email:	
	Signer's Signature:	

Service Performed:	Identification:		I.D. Number:	
☐ Oath	☐ I.D Card	☐ Credible Witness		
☐ Acknowledgment	☐ Drivers License	☐ Known Personally	Issued By:	
☐ Jurat	☐ Passport			
☐ Other:	☐ Other:		Issued Date:	Expiration Date:
Document Type:	Date/Time Notarized:	AM PM	Document Date:	Fee Charged:

Printed Name and Address of Witness:	Phone Number:
	Email:
	Witness' Signature:

Comments :	Record Number:

NOTARY RECORD

Printed Name and Address of Signer:	Phone Number:	Thumb Print:
	Email:	
	Signer's Signature:	

Service Performed:	Identification:		I.D. Number:	
☐ Oath	☐ I.D Card	☐ Credible Witness	Issued By:	
☐ Acknowledgment	☐ Drivers License	☐ Known Personally	Issued Date:	Expiration Date:
☐ Jurat	☐ Passport			
☐ Other:	☐ Other:			
Document Type:	Date/Time Notarized: AM PM		Document Date:	Fee Charged:

Printed Name and Address of Witness:	Phone Number:
	Email:
	Witness' Signature:

Comments :	Record Number:

NOTARY RECORD

Printed Name and Address of Signer:	Phone Number:	Thumb Print:
	Email:	
	Signer's Signature:	

Service Performed:	Identification:		I.D. Number:	
☐ Oath	☐ I.D Card	☐ Credible Witness	Issued By:	
☐ Acknowledgment	☐ Drivers License	☐ Known Personally	Issued Date:	Expiration Date:
☐ Jurat	☐ Passport			
☐ Other:	☐ Other:			
Document Type:	Date/Time Notarized: AM PM		Document Date:	Fee Charged:

Printed Name and Address of Witness:	Phone Number:
	Email:
	Witness' Signature:

Comments :	Record Number:

NOTARY RECORD

Printed Name and Address of Signer:	**Phone Number:**	**Thumb Print:**
	Email:	
	Signer's Signature:	

Service Performed: ☐ Oath ☐ Acknowledgment ☐ Jurat ☐ Other:	**Identification:** ☐ I.D Card ☐ Credible Witness ☐ Drivers License ☐ Known Personally ☐ Passport ☐ Other:	**I.D. Number:**	
		Issued By:	
		Issued Date:	**Expiration Date:**
Document Type:	**Date/Time Notarized:** AM PM	**Document Date:**	**Fee Charged:**

Printed Name and Address of Witness:	**Phone Number:**
	Email:
	Witness' Signature:
Comments :	**Record Number:**

NOTARY RECORD

Printed Name and Address of Signer:	**Phone Number:**	**Thumb Print:**
	Email:	
	Signer's Signature:	

Service Performed: ☐ Oath ☐ Acknowledgment ☐ Jurat ☐ Other:	**Identification:** ☐ I.D Card ☐ Credible Witness ☐ Drivers License ☐ Known Personally ☐ Passport ☐ Other:	**I.D. Number:**	
		Issued By:	
		Issued Date:	**Expiration Date:**
Document Type:	**Date/Time Notarized:** AM PM	**Document Date:**	**Fee Charged:**

Printed Name and Address of Witness:	**Phone Number:**
	Email:
	Witness' Signature:
Comments :	**Record Number:**

NOTARY RECORD

Printed Name and Address of Signer:	Phone Number:	Thumb Print:
	Email:	
	Signer's Signature:	

Service Performed:	Identification:		I.D. Number:	
☐ Oath	☐ I.D Card	☐ Credible Witness		
☐ Acknowledgment	☐ Drivers License	☐ Known Personally	Issued By:	
☐ Jurat	☐ Passport		Issued Date:	Expiration Date:
☐ Other:	☐ Other:			
Document Type:	Date/Time Notarized:	AM PM	Document Date:	Fee Charged:

Printed Name and Address of Witness:	Phone Number:
	Email:
	Witness' Signature:

Comments :	Record Number:

NOTARY RECORD

Printed Name and Address of Signer:	Phone Number:	Thumb Print:
	Email:	
	Signer's Signature:	

Service Performed:	Identification:		I.D. Number:	
☐ Oath	☐ I.D Card	☐ Credible Witness		
☐ Acknowledgment	☐ Drivers License	☐ Known Personally	Issued By:	
☐ Jurat	☐ Passport		Issued Date:	Expiration Date:
☐ Other:	☐ Other:			
Document Type:	Date/Time Notarized:	AM PM	Document Date:	Fee Charged:

Printed Name and Address of Witness:	Phone Number:
	Email:
	Witness' Signature:

Comments :	Record Number:

NOTARY RECORD

Printed Name and Address of Signer:

Phone Number:

Email:

Signer's Signature:

Thumb Print:

Service Performed:

- ☐ Oath
- ☐ Acknowledgment
- ☐ Jurat
- ☐ Other:

Identification:

- ☐ I.D Card
- ☐ Credible Witness
- ☐ Drivers License
- ☐ Known Personally
- ☐ Passport
- ☐ Other:

I.D. Number:

Issued By:

Issued Date:

Expiration Date:

Document Type:

Date/Time Notarized: **AM PM**

Document Date:

Fee Charged:

Printed Name and Address of Witness:

Phone Number:

Email:

Witness' Signature:

Comments :

Record Number:

NOTARY RECORD

Printed Name and Address of Signer:

Phone Number:

Email:

Signer's Signature:

Thumb Print:

Service Performed:

- ☐ Oath
- ☐ Acknowledgment
- ☐ Jurat
- ☐ Other:

Identification:

- ☐ I.D Card
- ☐ Credible Witness
- ☐ Drivers License
- ☐ Known Personally
- ☐ Passport
- ☐ Other:

I.D. Number:

Issued By:

Issued Date:

Expiration Date:

Document Type:

Date/Time Notarized: **AM PM**

Document Date:

Fee Charged:

Printed Name and Address of Witness:

Phone Number:

Email:

Witness' Signature:

Comments :

Record Number:

NOTARY RECORD

Printed Name and Address of Signer:	Phone Number:	Thumb Print:
	Email:	
	Signer's Signature:	

Service Performed:	Identification:		I.D. Number:	
☐ Oath	☐ I.D Card	☐ Credible Witness	Issued By:	
☐ Acknowledgment	☐ Drivers License	☐ Known Personally	Issued Date:	Expiration Date:
☐ Jurat	☐ Passport			
☐ Other:	☐ Other:			
Document Type:	Date/Time Notarized: AM PM		Document Date:	Fee Charged:

Printed Name and Address of Witness:	Phone Number:
	Email:
	Witness' Signature:

Comments :	Record Number:

NOTARY RECORD

Printed Name and Address of Signer:	Phone Number:	Thumb Print:
	Email:	
	Signer's Signature:	

Service Performed:	Identification:		I.D. Number:	
☐ Oath	☐ I.D Card	☐ Credible Witness	Issued By:	
☐ Acknowledgment	☐ Drivers License	☐ Known Personally	Issued Date:	Expiration Date:
☐ Jurat	☐ Passport			
☐ Other:	☐ Other:			
Document Type:	Date/Time Notarized: AM PM		Document Date:	Fee Charged:

Printed Name and Address of Witness:	Phone Number:
	Email:
	Witness' Signature:

Comments :	Record Number:

NOTARY RECORD

Printed Name and Address of Signer:	Phone Number:	Thumb Print:
	Email:	
	Signer's Signature:	

Service Performed:	Identification:		I.D. Number:	
☐ Oath	☐ I.D Card	☐ Credible Witness	Issued By:	
☐ Acknowledgment	☐ Drivers License	☐ Known Personally		
☐ Jurat	☐ Passport		Issued Date:	Expiration Date:
☐ Other:	☐ Other:			
Document Type:	Date/Time Notarized: AM PM		Document Date:	Fee Charged:

Printed Name and Address of Witness:	Phone Number:
	Email:
	Witness' Signature:

Comments :	Record Number:

NOTARY RECORD

Printed Name and Address of Signer:	Phone Number:	Thumb Print:
	Email:	
	Signer's Signature:	

Service Performed:	Identification:		I.D. Number:	
☐ Oath	☐ I.D Card	☐ Credible Witness	Issued By:	
☐ Acknowledgment	☐ Drivers License	☐ Known Personally		
☐ Jurat	☐ Passport		Issued Date:	Expiration Date:
☐ Other:	☐ Other:			
Document Type:	Date/Time Notarized: AM PM		Document Date:	Fee Charged:

Printed Name and Address of Witness:	Phone Number:
	Email:
	Witness' Signature:

Comments :	Record Number:

NOTARY RECORD

Printed Name and Address of Signer:	**Phone Number:**	**Thumb Print:**
	Email:	
	Signer's Signature:	

Service Performed: ☐ Oath ☐ Acknowledgment ☐ Jurat ☐ Other:	**Identification:** ☐ I.D Card ☐ Credible Witness ☐ Drivers License ☐ Known Personally ☐ Passport ☐ Other:	**I.D. Number:**	
		Issued By:	
		Issued Date:	**Expiration Date:**
Document Type:	**Date/Time Notarized:** AM PM	**Document Date:**	**Fee Charged:**

Printed Name and Address of Witness:	**Phone Number:**
	Email:
	Witness' Signature:
Comments :	**Record Number:**

NOTARY RECORD

Printed Name and Address of Signer:	**Phone Number:**	**Thumb Print:**
	Email:	
	Signer's Signature:	

Service Performed: ☐ Oath ☐ Acknowledgment ☐ Jurat ☐ Other:	**Identification:** ☐ I.D Card ☐ Credible Witness ☐ Drivers License ☐ Known Personally ☐ Passport ☐ Other:	**I.D. Number:**	
		Issued By:	
		Issued Date:	**Expiration Date:**
Document Type:	**Date/Time Notarized:** AM PM	**Document Date:**	**Fee Charged:**

Printed Name and Address of Witness:	**Phone Number:**
	Email:
	Witness' Signature:
Comments :	**Record Number:**

NOTARY RECORD

Printed Name and Address of Signer:	Phone Number:	Thumb Print:
	Email:	
	Signer's Signature:	

Service Performed:	Identification:		I.D. Number:	
☐ Oath	☐ I.D Card	☐ Credible Witness	Issued By:	
☐ Acknowledgment	☐ Drivers License	☐ Known Personally		
☐ Jurat	☐ Passport		Issued Date:	Expiration Date:
☐ Other:	☐ Other:			
Document Type:	Date/Time Notarized: AM PM		Document Date:	Fee Charged:

Printed Name and Address of Witness:	Phone Number:
	Email:
	Witness' Signature:

Comments :	Record Number:

NOTARY RECORD

Printed Name and Address of Signer:	Phone Number:	Thumb Print:
	Email:	
	Signer's Signature:	

Service Performed:	Identification:		I.D. Number:	
☐ Oath	☐ I.D Card	☐ Credible Witness	Issued By:	
☐ Acknowledgment	☐ Drivers License	☐ Known Personally		
☐ Jurat	☐ Passport		Issued Date:	Expiration Date:
☐ Other:	☐ Other:			
Document Type:	Date/Time Notarized: AM PM		Document Date:	Fee Charged:

Printed Name and Address of Witness:	Phone Number:
	Email:
	Witness' Signature:

Comments :	Record Number:

NOTARY RECORD

Printed Name and Address of Signer:	Phone Number:	Thumb Print:
	Email:	
	Signer's Signature:	

Service Performed:	Identification:		I.D. Number:	
☐ Oath	☐ I.D Card	☐ Credible Witness		
☐ Acknowledgment	☐ Drivers License	☐ Known Personally	Issued By:	
☐ Jurat	☐ Passport			
☐ Other:	☐ Other:		Issued Date:	Expiration Date:
Document Type:	Date/Time Notarized: AM PM		Document Date:	Fee Charged:

Printed Name and Address of Witness:	Phone Number:
	Email:
	Witness' Signature:

Comments :	Record Number:

NOTARY RECORD

Printed Name and Address of Signer:	Phone Number:	Thumb Print:
	Email:	
	Signer's Signature:	

Service Performed:	Identification:		I.D. Number:	
☐ Oath	☐ I.D Card	☐ Credible Witness		
☐ Acknowledgment	☐ Drivers License	☐ Known Personally	Issued By:	
☐ Jurat	☐ Passport			
☐ Other:	☐ Other:		Issued Date:	Expiration Date:
Document Type:	Date/Time Notarized: AM PM		Document Date:	Fee Charged:

Printed Name and Address of Witness:	Phone Number:
	Email:
	Witness' Signature:

Comments :	Record Number:

NOTARY RECORD

Printed Name and Address of Signer:	**Phone Number:** **Email:** **Signer's Signature:**	**Thumb Print:**

Service Performed: ☐ Oath ☐ Acknowledgment ☐ Jurat ☐ Other:	**Identification:** ☐ I.D Card ☐ Credible Witness ☐ Drivers License ☐ Known Personally ☐ Passport ☐ Other:	**I.D. Number:** **Issued By:** **Issued Date:**	**Expiration Date:**
Document Type:	**Date/Time Notarized:** AM PM	**Document Date:**	**Fee Charged:**

Printed Name and Address of Witness:	**Phone Number:** **Email:** **Witness' Signature:**
Comments :	**Record Number:**

NOTARY RECORD

Printed Name and Address of Signer:	**Phone Number:** **Email:** **Signer's Signature:**	**Thumb Print:**

Service Performed: ☐ Oath ☐ Acknowledgment ☐ Jurat ☐ Other:	**Identification:** ☐ I.D Card ☐ Credible Witness ☐ Drivers License ☐ Known Personally ☐ Passport ☐ Other:	**I.D. Number:** **Issued By:** **Issued Date:**	**Expiration Date:**
Document Type:	**Date/Time Notarized:** AM PM	**Document Date:**	**Fee Charged:**

Printed Name and Address of Witness:	**Phone Number:** **Email:** **Witness' Signature:**
Comments :	**Record Number:**

NOTARY RECORD

Printed Name and Address of Signer:	Phone Number:	Thumb Print:
	Email:	
	Signer's Signature:	

Service Performed:	Identification:		I.D. Number:	
☐ Oath	☐ I.D Card	☐ Credible Witness	Issued By:	
☐ Acknowledgment	☐ Drivers License	☐ Known Personally	Issued Date:	Expiration Date:
☐ Jurat	☐ Passport			
☐ Other:	☐ Other:			
Document Type:	Date/Time Notarized: AM PM		Document Date:	Fee Charged:

Printed Name and Address of Witness:	Phone Number:
	Email:
	Witness' Signature:

Comments :	Record Number:

NOTARY RECORD

Printed Name and Address of Signer:	Phone Number:	Thumb Print:
	Email:	
	Signer's Signature:	

Service Performed:	Identification:		I.D. Number:	
☐ Oath	☐ I.D Card	☐ Credible Witness	Issued By:	
☐ Acknowledgment	☐ Drivers License	☐ Known Personally	Issued Date:	Expiration Date:
☐ Jurat	☐ Passport			
☐ Other:	☐ Other:			
Document Type:	Date/Time Notarized: AM PM		Document Date:	Fee Charged:

Printed Name and Address of Witness:	Phone Number:
	Email:
	Witness' Signature:

Comments :	Record Number:

NOTARY RECORD

Printed Name and Address of Signer:	**Phone Number:**	**Thumb Print:**
	Email:	
	Signer's Signature:	

Service Performed: ☐ Oath ☐ Acknowledgment ☐ Jurat ☐ Other:	**Identification:** ☐ I.D Card ☐ Credible Witness ☐ Drivers License ☐ Known Personally ☐ Passport ☐ Other:	**I.D. Number:**	
		Issued By:	
		Issued Date:	**Expiration Date:**
Document Type:	**Date/Time Notarized:** AM PM	**Document Date:**	**Fee Charged:**

Printed Name and Address of Witness:	**Phone Number:**
	Email:
	Witness' Signature:

Comments :	**Record Number:**

NOTARY RECORD

Printed Name and Address of Signer:	**Phone Number:**	**Thumb Print:**
	Email:	
	Signer's Signature:	

Service Performed: ☐ Oath ☐ Acknowledgment ☐ Jurat ☐ Other:	**Identification:** ☐ I.D Card ☐ Credible Witness ☐ Drivers License ☐ Known Personally ☐ Passport ☐ Other:	**I.D. Number:**	
		Issued By:	
		Issued Date:	**Expiration Date:**
Document Type:	**Date/Time Notarized:** AM PM	**Document Date:**	**Fee Charged:**

Printed Name and Address of Witness:	**Phone Number:**
	Email:
	Witness' Signature:

Comments :	**Record Number:**

NOTARY RECORD

Printed Name and Address of Signer:	Phone Number:	Thumb Print:
	Email:	
	Signer's Signature:	

Service Performed:	Identification:		I.D. Number:	
☐ Oath	☐ I.D Card	☐ Credible Witness	Issued By:	
☐ Acknowledgment	☐ Drivers License	☐ Known Personally	Issued Date:	Expiration Date:
☐ Jurat	☐ Passport			
☐ Other:	☐ Other:			
Document Type:	Date/Time Notarized:	AM PM	Document Date:	Fee Charged:

Printed Name and Address of Witness:	Phone Number:
	Email:
	Witness' Signature:

Comments :	Record Number:

NOTARY RECORD

Printed Name and Address of Signer:	Phone Number:	Thumb Print:
	Email:	
	Signer's Signature:	

Service Performed:	Identification:		I.D. Number:	
☐ Oath	☐ I.D Card	☐ Credible Witness	Issued By:	
☐ Acknowledgment	☐ Drivers License	☐ Known Personally	Issued Date:	Expiration Date:
☐ Jurat	☐ Passport			
☐ Other:	☐ Other:			
Document Type:	Date/Time Notarized:	AM PM	Document Date:	Fee Charged:

Printed Name and Address of Witness:	Phone Number:
	Email:
	Witness' Signature:

Comments :	Record Number:

NOTARY RECORD

Printed Name and Address of Signer:	Phone Number:	Thumb Print:
	Email:	
	Signer's Signature:	

Service Performed:	Identification:		I.D. Number:	
☐ Oath	☐ I.D Card	☐ Credible Witness	Issued By:	
☐ Acknowledgment	☐ Drivers License	☐ Known Personally		
☐ Jurat	☐ Passport		Issued Date:	Expiration Date:
☐ Other:	☐ Other:			
Document Type:	Date/Time Notarized: AM PM		Document Date:	Fee Charged:

Printed Name and Address of Witness:	Phone Number:
	Email:
	Witness' Signature:

Comments :	Record Number:

NOTARY RECORD

Printed Name and Address of Signer:	Phone Number:	Thumb Print:
	Email:	
	Signer's Signature:	

Service Performed:	Identification:		I.D. Number:	
☐ Oath	☐ I.D Card	☐ Credible Witness	Issued By:	
☐ Acknowledgment	☐ Drivers License	☐ Known Personally		
☐ Jurat	☐ Passport		Issued Date:	Expiration Date:
☐ Other:	☐ Other:			
Document Type:	Date/Time Notarized: AM PM		Document Date:	Fee Charged:

Printed Name and Address of Witness:	Phone Number:
	Email:
	Witness' Signature:

Comments :	Record Number:

NOTARY RECORD

Printed Name and Address of Signer:	Phone Number:	Thumb Print:
	Email:	
	Signer's Signature:	

Service Performed:	Identification:		I.D. Number:	
☐ Oath	☐ I.D Card	☐ Credible Witness	Issued By:	
☐ Acknowledgment	☐ Drivers License	☐ Known Personally		
☐ Jurat	☐ Passport		Issued Date:	Expiration Date:
☐ Other:	☐ Other:			
Document Type:	Date/Time Notarized:	AM PM	Document Date:	Fee Charged:

Printed Name and Address of Witness:	Phone Number:
	Email:
	Witness' Signature:

Comments :	Record Number:

NOTARY RECORD

Printed Name and Address of Signer:	Phone Number:	Thumb Print:
	Email:	
	Signer's Signature:	

Service Performed:	Identification:		I.D. Number:	
☐ Oath	☐ I.D Card	☐ Credible Witness	Issued By:	
☐ Acknowledgment	☐ Drivers License	☐ Known Personally		
☐ Jurat	☐ Passport		Issued Date:	Expiration Date:
☐ Other:	☐ Other:			
Document Type:	Date/Time Notarized:	AM PM	Document Date:	Fee Charged:

Printed Name and Address of Witness:	Phone Number:
	Email:
	Witness' Signature:

Comments :	Record Number:

NOTARY RECORD

Printed Name and Address of Signer:	**Phone Number:**	**Thumb Print:**
	Email:	
	Signer's Signature:	

Service Performed: ☐ Oath ☐ Acknowledgment ☐ Jurat ☐ Other:	**Identification:** ☐ I.D Card ☐ Credible Witness ☐ Drivers License ☐ Known Personally ☐ Passport ☐ Other:	**I.D. Number:**	
		Issued By:	
		Issued Date:	**Expiration Date:**
Document Type:	**Date/Time Notarized:** AM PM	**Document Date:**	**Fee Charged:**

Printed Name and Address of Witness:	**Phone Number:**
	Email:
	Witness' Signature:

Comments :	**Record Number:**

NOTARY RECORD

Printed Name and Address of Signer:	**Phone Number:**	**Thumb Print:**
	Email:	
	Signer's Signature:	

Service Performed: ☐ Oath ☐ Acknowledgment ☐ Jurat ☐ Other:	**Identification:** ☐ I.D Card ☐ Credible Witness ☐ Drivers License ☐ Known Personally ☐ Passport ☐ Other:	**I.D. Number:**	
		Issued By:	
		Issued Date:	**Expiration Date:**
Document Type:	**Date/Time Notarized:** AM PM	**Document Date:**	**Fee Charged:**

Printed Name and Address of Witness:	**Phone Number:**
	Email:
	Witness' Signature:

Comments :	**Record Number:**

NOTARY RECORD

Printed Name and Address of Signer:	Phone Number:	Thumb Print:
	Email:	
	Signer's Signature:	

Service Performed:	Identification:		I.D. Number:	
☐ Oath	☐ I.D Card	☐ Credible Witness		
☐ Acknowledgment	☐ Drivers License	☐ Known Personally	Issued By:	
☐ Jurat	☐ Passport			
☐ Other:	☐ Other:		Issued Date:	Expiration Date:
Document Type:	Date/Time Notarized: AM PM		Document Date:	Fee Charged:

Printed Name and Address of Witness:	Phone Number:
	Email:
	Witness' Signature:

Comments :	Record Number:

NOTARY RECORD

Printed Name and Address of Signer:	Phone Number:	Thumb Print:
	Email:	
	Signer's Signature:	

Service Performed:	Identification:		I.D. Number:	
☐ Oath	☐ I.D Card	☐ Credible Witness		
☐ Acknowledgment	☐ Drivers License	☐ Known Personally	Issued By:	
☐ Jurat	☐ Passport			
☐ Other:	☐ Other:		Issued Date:	Expiration Date:
Document Type:	Date/Time Notarized: AM PM		Document Date:	Fee Charged:

Printed Name and Address of Witness:	Phone Number:
	Email:
	Witness' Signature:

Comments :	Record Number:

NOTARY RECORD

Printed Name and Address of Signer:	**Phone Number:**	**Thumb Print:**
	Email:	
	Signer's Signature:	

Service Performed: ☐ Oath ☐ Acknowledgment ☐ Jurat ☐ Other:	**Identification:** ☐ I.D Card ☐ Credible Witness ☐ Drivers License ☐ Known Personally ☐ Passport ☐ Other:	**I.D. Number:**	
		Issued By:	
		Issued Date:	**Expiration Date:**
Document Type:	**Date/Time Notarized:** AM PM	**Document Date:**	**Fee Charged:**

Printed Name and Address of Witness:	**Phone Number:**
	Email:
	Witness' Signature:
Comments :	**Record Number:**

NOTARY RECORD

Printed Name and Address of Signer:	**Phone Number:**	**Thumb Print:**
	Email:	
	Signer's Signature:	

Service Performed: ☐ Oath ☐ Acknowledgment ☐ Jurat ☐ Other:	**Identification:** ☐ I.D Card ☐ Credible Witness ☐ Drivers License ☐ Known Personally ☐ Passport ☐ Other:	**I.D. Number:**	
		Issued By:	
		Issued Date:	**Expiration Date:**
Document Type:	**Date/Time Notarized:** AM PM	**Document Date:**	**Fee Charged:**

Printed Name and Address of Witness:	**Phone Number:**
	Email:
	Witness' Signature:
Comments :	**Record Number:**

NOTARY RECORD

Printed Name and Address of Signer:	**Phone Number:**	**Thumb Print:**
	Email:	
	Signer's Signature:	

Service Performed: ☐ Oath ☐ Acknowledgment ☐ Jurat ☐ Other:	**Identification:** ☐ I.D Card ☐ Credible Witness ☐ Drivers License ☐ Known Personally ☐ Passport ☐ Other:	**I.D. Number:**	
		Issued By:	
		Issued Date:	**Expiration Date:**
Document Type:	**Date/Time Notarized:** AM PM	**Document Date:**	**Fee Charged:**

Printed Name and Address of Witness:	**Phone Number:**
	Email:
	Witness' Signature:
Comments :	**Record Number:**

NOTARY RECORD

Printed Name and Address of Signer:	**Phone Number:**	**Thumb Print:**
	Email:	
	Signer's Signature:	

Service Performed: ☐ Oath ☐ Acknowledgment ☐ Jurat ☐ Other:	**Identification:** ☐ I.D Card ☐ Credible Witness ☐ Drivers License ☐ Known Personally ☐ Passport ☐ Other:	**I.D. Number:**	
		Issued By:	
		Issued Date:	**Expiration Date:**
Document Type:	**Date/Time Notarized:** AM PM	**Document Date:**	**Fee Charged:**

Printed Name and Address of Witness:	**Phone Number:**
	Email:
	Witness' Signature:
Comments :	**Record Number:**

NOTARY RECORD

Printed Name and Address of Signer:	**Phone Number:**	**Thumb Print:**
	Email:	
	Signer's Signature:	

Service Performed: ☐ Oath ☐ Acknowledgment ☐ Jurat ☐ Other:	**Identification:** ☐ I.D Card ☐ Credible Witness ☐ Drivers License ☐ Known Personally ☐ Passport ☐ Other:	**I.D. Number:**	
		Issued By:	
		Issued Date:	**Expiration Date:**
Document Type:	**Date/Time Notarized:** AM PM	**Document Date:**	**Fee Charged:**

Printed Name and Address of Witness:	**Phone Number:**
	Email:
	Witness' Signature:

Comments :	**Record Number:**

NOTARY RECORD

Printed Name and Address of Signer:	**Phone Number:**	**Thumb Print:**
	Email:	
	Signer's Signature:	

Service Performed: ☐ Oath ☐ Acknowledgment ☐ Jurat ☐ Other:	**Identification:** ☐ I.D Card ☐ Credible Witness ☐ Drivers License ☐ Known Personally ☐ Passport ☐ Other:	**I.D. Number:**	
		Issued By:	
		Issued Date:	**Expiration Date:**
Document Type:	**Date/Time Notarized:** AM PM	**Document Date:**	**Fee Charged:**

Printed Name and Address of Witness:	**Phone Number:**
	Email:
	Witness' Signature:

Comments :	**Record Number:**

NOTARY RECORD

Printed Name and Address of Signer:	Phone Number:	Thumb Print:
	Email:	
	Signer's Signature:	

Service Performed:	Identification:		I.D. Number:	
☐ Oath	☐ I.D Card	☐ Credible Witness	Issued By:	
☐ Acknowledgment	☐ Drivers License	☐ Known Personally	Issued Date:	Expiration Date:
☐ Jurat	☐ Passport			
☐ Other:	☐ Other:			
Document Type:	Date/Time Notarized: AM PM		Document Date:	Fee Charged:

Printed Name and Address of Witness:	Phone Number:
	Email:
	Witness' Signature:

Comments :	Record Number:

NOTARY RECORD

Printed Name and Address of Signer:	Phone Number:	Thumb Print:
	Email:	
	Signer's Signature:	

Service Performed:	Identification:		I.D. Number:	
☐ Oath	☐ I.D Card	☐ Credible Witness	Issued By:	
☐ Acknowledgment	☐ Drivers License	☐ Known Personally	Issued Date:	Expiration Date:
☐ Jurat	☐ Passport			
☐ Other:	☐ Other:			
Document Type:	Date/Time Notarized: AM PM		Document Date:	Fee Charged:

Printed Name and Address of Witness:	Phone Number:
	Email:
	Witness' Signature:

Comments :	Record Number:

NOTARY RECORD

Printed Name and Address of Signer:	**Phone Number:**	**Thumb Print:**
	Email:	
	Signer's Signature:	

Service Performed: ☐ Oath ☐ Acknowledgment ☐ Jurat ☐ Other:	**Identification:** ☐ I.D Card ☐ Credible Witness ☐ Drivers License ☐ Known Personally ☐ Passport ☐ Other:	**I.D. Number:**	
		Issued By:	
		Issued Date:	**Expiration Date:**
Document Type:	**Date/Time Notarized:** AM PM	**Document Date:**	**Fee Charged:**

Printed Name and Address of Witness:	**Phone Number:**
	Email:
	Witness' Signature:

Comments :	**Record Number:**

NOTARY RECORD

Printed Name and Address of Signer:	**Phone Number:**	**Thumb Print:**
	Email:	
	Signer's Signature:	

Service Performed: ☐ Oath ☐ Acknowledgment ☐ Jurat ☐ Other:	**Identification:** ☐ I.D Card ☐ Credible Witness ☐ Drivers License ☐ Known Personally ☐ Passport ☐ Other:	**I.D. Number:**	
		Issued By:	
		Issued Date:	**Expiration Date:**
Document Type:	**Date/Time Notarized:** AM PM	**Document Date:**	**Fee Charged:**

Printed Name and Address of Witness:	**Phone Number:**
	Email:
	Witness' Signature:

Comments :	**Record Number:**

NOTARY RECORD

Printed Name and Address of Signer:	Phone Number:	Thumb Print:
	Email:	
	Signer's Signature:	

Service Performed:	Identification:		I.D. Number:	
☐ Oath	☐ I.D Card	☐ Credible Witness		
☐ Acknowledgment	☐ Drivers License	☐ Known Personally	Issued By:	
☐ Jurat	☐ Passport			
☐ Other:	☐ Other:		Issued Date:	Expiration Date:
Document Type:	Date/Time Notarized: AM PM		Document Date:	Fee Charged:

Printed Name and Address of Witness:	Phone Number:
	Email:
	Witness' Signature:

Comments :	Record Number:

NOTARY RECORD

Printed Name and Address of Signer:	Phone Number:	Thumb Print:
	Email:	
	Signer's Signature:	

Service Performed:	Identification:		I.D. Number:	
☐ Oath	☐ I.D Card	☐ Credible Witness		
☐ Acknowledgment	☐ Drivers License	☐ Known Personally	Issued By:	
☐ Jurat	☐ Passport			
☐ Other:	☐ Other:		Issued Date:	Expiration Date:
Document Type:	Date/Time Notarized: AM PM		Document Date:	Fee Charged:

Printed Name and Address of Witness:	Phone Number:
	Email:
	Witness' Signature:

Comments :	Record Number:

NOTARY RECORD

Printed Name and Address of Signer:

Phone Number:

Email:

Signer's Signature:

Thumb Print:

Service Performed:

- ☐ Oath
- ☐ Acknowledgment
- ☐ Jurat
- ☐ Other:

Identification:

- ☐ I.D Card
- ☐ Credible Witness
- ☐ Drivers License
- ☐ Known Personally
- ☐ Passport
- ☐ Other:

I.D. Number:

Issued By:

Issued Date:

Expiration Date:

Document Type:

Date/Time Notarized: AM PM

Document Date:

Fee Charged:

Printed Name and Address of Witness:

Phone Number:

Email:

Witness' Signature:

Comments :

Record Number:

NOTARY RECORD

Printed Name and Address of Signer:

Phone Number:

Email:

Signer's Signature:

Thumb Print:

Service Performed:

- ☐ Oath
- ☐ Acknowledgment
- ☐ Jurat
- ☐ Other:

Identification:

- ☐ I.D Card
- ☐ Credible Witness
- ☐ Drivers License
- ☐ Known Personally
- ☐ Passport
- ☐ Other:

I.D. Number:

Issued By:

Issued Date:

Expiration Date:

Document Type:

Date/Time Notarized: AM PM

Document Date:

Fee Charged:

Printed Name and Address of Witness:

Phone Number:

Email:

Witness' Signature:

Comments :

Record Number:

NOTARY RECORD

Printed Name and Address of Signer:	**Phone Number:**	**Thumb Print:**
	Email:	
	Signer's Signature:	

Service Performed: ☐ Oath ☐ Acknowledgment ☐ Jurat ☐ Other:	**Identification:** ☐ I.D Card ☐ Credible Witness ☐ Drivers License ☐ Known Personally ☐ Passport ☐ Other:	**I.D. Number:**	
		Issued By:	
		Issued Date:	**Expiration Date:**
Document Type:	**Date/Time Notarized:** AM PM	**Document Date:**	**Fee Charged:**

Printed Name and Address of Witness:	**Phone Number:**
	Email:
	Witness' Signature:
Comments :	**Record Number:**

NOTARY RECORD

Printed Name and Address of Signer:	**Phone Number:**	**Thumb Print:**
	Email:	
	Signer's Signature:	

Service Performed: ☐ Oath ☐ Acknowledgment ☐ Jurat ☐ Other:	**Identification:** ☐ I.D Card ☐ Credible Witness ☐ Drivers License ☐ Known Personally ☐ Passport ☐ Other:	**I.D. Number:**	
		Issued By:	
		Issued Date:	**Expiration Date:**
Document Type:	**Date/Time Notarized:** AM PM	**Document Date:**	**Fee Charged:**

Printed Name and Address of Witness:	**Phone Number:**
	Email:
	Witness' Signature:
Comments :	**Record Number:**

NOTARY RECORD

Printed Name and Address of Signer:	Phone Number:	Thumb Print:
	Email:	
	Signer's Signature:	

Service Performed:	Identification:		I.D. Number:	
☐ Oath	☐ I.D Card	☐ Credible Witness	Issued By:	
☐ Acknowledgment	☐ Drivers License	☐ Known Personally		
☐ Jurat	☐ Passport		Issued Date:	Expiration Date:
☐ Other:	☐ Other:			
Document Type:	Date/Time Notarized: AM PM		Document Date:	Fee Charged:

Printed Name and Address of Witness:	Phone Number:
	Email:
	Witness' Signature:

Comments :	Record Number:

NOTARY RECORD

Printed Name and Address of Signer:	Phone Number:	Thumb Print:
	Email:	
	Signer's Signature:	

Service Performed:	Identification:		I.D. Number:	
☐ Oath	☐ I.D Card	☐ Credible Witness	Issued By:	
☐ Acknowledgment	☐ Drivers License	☐ Known Personally		
☐ Jurat	☐ Passport		Issued Date:	Expiration Date:
☐ Other:	☐ Other:			
Document Type:	Date/Time Notarized: AM PM		Document Date:	Fee Charged:

Printed Name and Address of Witness:	Phone Number:
	Email:
	Witness' Signature:

Comments :	Record Number:

NOTARY RECORD

Printed Name and Address of Signer:	Phone Number:	Thumb Print:
	Email:	
	Signer's Signature:	

Service Performed:	Identification:		I.D. Number:	
☐ Oath	☐ I.D Card	☐ Credible Witness	Issued By:	
☐ Acknowledgment	☐ Drivers License	☐ Known Personally	Issued Date:	Expiration Date:
☐ Jurat	☐ Passport			
☐ Other:	☐ Other:			
Document Type:	Date/Time Notarized: AM PM		Document Date:	Fee Charged:

Printed Name and Address of Witness:	Phone Number:
	Email:
	Witness' Signature:

Comments :	Record Number:

NOTARY RECORD

Printed Name and Address of Signer:	Phone Number:	Thumb Print:
	Email:	
	Signer's Signature:	

Service Performed:	Identification:		I.D. Number:	
☐ Oath	☐ I.D Card	☐ Credible Witness	Issued By:	
☐ Acknowledgment	☐ Drivers License	☐ Known Personally	Issued Date:	Expiration Date:
☐ Jurat	☐ Passport			
☐ Other:	☐ Other:			
Document Type:	Date/Time Notarized: AM PM		Document Date:	Fee Charged:

Printed Name and Address of Witness:	Phone Number:
	Email:
	Witness' Signature:

Comments :	Record Number:

NOTARY RECORD

Printed Name and Address of Signer:	**Phone Number:**	**Thumb Print:**
	Email:	
	Signer's Signature:	

Service Performed: ☐ Oath ☐ Acknowledgment ☐ Jurat ☐ Other:	**Identification:** ☐ I.D Card ☐ Credible Witness ☐ Drivers License ☐ Known Personally ☐ Passport ☐ Other:	**I.D. Number:**	
		Issued By:	
		Issued Date:	**Expiration Date:**
Document Type:	**Date/Time Notarized:** AM PM	**Document Date:**	**Fee Charged:**

Printed Name and Address of Witness:	**Phone Number:**
	Email:
	Witness' Signature:
Comments :	**Record Number:**

NOTARY RECORD

Printed Name and Address of Signer:	**Phone Number:**	**Thumb Print:**
	Email:	
	Signer's Signature:	

Service Performed: ☐ Oath ☐ Acknowledgment ☐ Jurat ☐ Other:	**Identification:** ☐ I.D Card ☐ Credible Witness ☐ Drivers License ☐ Known Personally ☐ Passport ☐ Other:	**I.D. Number:**	
		Issued By:	
		Issued Date:	**Expiration Date:**
Document Type:	**Date/Time Notarized:** AM PM	**Document Date:**	**Fee Charged:**

Printed Name and Address of Witness:	**Phone Number:**
	Email:
	Witness' Signature:
Comments :	**Record Number:**

NOTARY RECORD

Printed Name and Address of Signer:	Phone Number:	Thumb Print:
	Email:	
	Signer's Signature:	

Service Performed:	Identification:		I.D. Number:	
☐ Oath	☐ I.D Card	☐ Credible Witness	Issued By:	
☐ Acknowledgment	☐ Drivers License	☐ Known Personally	Issued Date:	Expiration Date:
☐ Jurat	☐ Passport			
☐ Other:	☐ Other:			
Document Type:	Date/Time Notarized: AM PM		Document Date:	Fee Charged:

Printed Name and Address of Witness:	Phone Number:
	Email:
	Witness' Signature:

Comments :	Record Number:

NOTARY RECORD

Printed Name and Address of Signer:	Phone Number:	Thumb Print:
	Email:	
	Signer's Signature:	

Service Performed:	Identification:		I.D. Number:	
☐ Oath	☐ I.D Card	☐ Credible Witness	Issued By:	
☐ Acknowledgment	☐ Drivers License	☐ Known Personally	Issued Date:	Expiration Date:
☐ Jurat	☐ Passport			
☐ Other:	☐ Other:			
Document Type:	Date/Time Notarized: AM PM		Document Date:	Fee Charged:

Printed Name and Address of Witness:	Phone Number:
	Email:
	Witness' Signature:

Comments :	Record Number:

NOTARY RECORD

Printed Name and Address of Signer:	**Phone Number:**	**Thumb Print:**
	Email:	
	Signer's Signature:	

Service Performed: ☐ Oath ☐ Acknowledgment ☐ Jurat ☐ Other:	**Identification:** ☐ I.D Card ☐ Credible Witness ☐ Drivers License ☐ Known Personally ☐ Passport ☐ Other:	**I.D. Number:**	
		Issued By:	
		Issued Date:	**Expiration Date:**
Document Type:	**Date/Time Notarized:** AM PM	**Document Date:**	**Fee Charged:**

Printed Name and Address of Witness:	**Phone Number:**
	Email:
	Witness' Signature:

Comments :	**Record Number:**

NOTARY RECORD

Printed Name and Address of Signer:	**Phone Number:**	**Thumb Print:**
	Email:	
	Signer's Signature:	

Service Performed: ☐ Oath ☐ Acknowledgment ☐ Jurat ☐ Other:	**Identification:** ☐ I.D Card ☐ Credible Witness ☐ Drivers License ☐ Known Personally ☐ Passport ☐ Other:	**I.D. Number:**	
		Issued By:	
		Issued Date:	**Expiration Date:**
Document Type:	**Date/Time Notarized:** AM PM	**Document Date:**	**Fee Charged:**

Printed Name and Address of Witness:	**Phone Number:**
	Email:
	Witness' Signature:

Comments :	**Record Number:**

NOTARY RECORD

Printed Name and Address of Signer:	Phone Number:	Thumb Print:
	Email:	
	Signer's Signature:	

Service Performed:	Identification:		I.D. Number:	
☐ Oath	☐ I.D Card	☐ Credible Witness	Issued By:	
☐ Acknowledgment	☐ Drivers License	☐ Known Personally		
☐ Jurat	☐ Passport		Issued Date:	Expiration Date:
☐ Other:	☐ Other:			
Document Type:	Date/Time Notarized:	AM PM	Document Date:	Fee Charged:

Printed Name and Address of Witness:	Phone Number:
	Email:
	Witness' Signature:

Comments :	Record Number:

NOTARY RECORD

Printed Name and Address of Signer:	Phone Number:	Thumb Print:
	Email:	
	Signer's Signature:	

Service Performed:	Identification:		I.D. Number:	
☐ Oath	☐ I.D Card	☐ Credible Witness	Issued By:	
☐ Acknowledgment	☐ Drivers License	☐ Known Personally		
☐ Jurat	☐ Passport		Issued Date:	Expiration Date:
☐ Other:	☐ Other:			
Document Type:	Date/Time Notarized:	AM PM	Document Date:	Fee Charged:

Printed Name and Address of Witness:	Phone Number:
	Email:
	Witness' Signature:

Comments :	Record Number:

NOTARY RECORD

Printed Name and Address of Signer:

Phone Number:

Email:

Signer's Signature:

Thumb Print:

Service Performed:

- ☐ Oath
- ☐ Acknowledgment
- ☐ Jurat
- ☐ Other:

Identification:

- ☐ I.D Card
- ☐ Credible Witness
- ☐ Drivers License
- ☐ Known Personally
- ☐ Passport
- ☐ Other:

I.D. Number:

Issued By:

Issued Date:

Expiration Date:

Document Type:

Date/Time Notarized: **AM** **PM**

Document Date:

Fee Charged:

Printed Name and Address of Witness:

Phone Number:

Email:

Witness' Signature:

Comments :

Record Number:

NOTARY RECORD

Printed Name and Address of Signer:

Phone Number:

Email:

Signer's Signature:

Thumb Print:

Service Performed:

- ☐ Oath
- ☐ Acknowledgment
- ☐ Jurat
- ☐ Other:

Identification:

- ☐ I.D Card
- ☐ Credible Witness
- ☐ Drivers License
- ☐ Known Personally
- ☐ Passport
- ☐ Other:

I.D. Number:

Issued By:

Issued Date:

Expiration Date:

Document Type:

Date/Time Notarized: **AM** **PM**

Document Date:

Fee Charged:

Printed Name and Address of Witness:

Phone Number:

Email:

Witness' Signature:

Comments :

Record Number:

NOTARY RECORD

Printed Name and Address of Signer:	Phone Number:	Thumb Print:
	Email:	
	Signer's Signature:	

Service Performed:	Identification:		I.D. Number:	
☐ Oath	☐ I.D Card	☐ Credible Witness	Issued By:	
☐ Acknowledgment	☐ Drivers License	☐ Known Personally	Issued Date:	Expiration Date:
☐ Jurat	☐ Passport			
☐ Other:	☐ Other:			
Document Type:	Date/Time Notarized: AM PM		Document Date:	Fee Charged:

Printed Name and Address of Witness:	Phone Number:
	Email:
	Witness' Signature:

Comments :	Record Number:

NOTARY RECORD

Printed Name and Address of Signer:	Phone Number:	Thumb Print:
	Email:	
	Signer's Signature:	

Service Performed:	Identification:		I.D. Number:	
☐ Oath	☐ I.D Card	☐ Credible Witness	Issued By:	
☐ Acknowledgment	☐ Drivers License	☐ Known Personally	Issued Date:	Expiration Date:
☐ Jurat	☐ Passport			
☐ Other:	☐ Other:			
Document Type:	Date/Time Notarized: AM PM		Document Date:	Fee Charged:

Printed Name and Address of Witness:	Phone Number:
	Email:
	Witness' Signature:

Comments :	Record Number:

NOTARY RECORD

Printed Name and Address of Signer:

Phone Number:

Email:

Signer's Signature:

Thumb Print:

Service Performed:

- ☐ Oath
- ☐ Acknowledgment
- ☐ Jurat
- ☐ Other:

Identification:

- ☐ I.D Card
- ☐ Credible Witness
- ☐ Drivers License
- ☐ Known Personally
- ☐ Passport
- ☐ Other:

I.D. Number:

Issued By:

Issued Date:

Expiration Date:

Document Type:

Date/Time Notarized: **AM** **PM**

Document Date:

Fee Charged:

Printed Name and Address of Witness:

Phone Number:

Email:

Witness' Signature:

Comments :

Record Number:

NOTARY RECORD

Printed Name and Address of Signer:

Phone Number:

Email:

Signer's Signature:

Thumb Print:

Service Performed:

- ☐ Oath
- ☐ Acknowledgment
- ☐ Jurat
- ☐ Other:

Identification:

- ☐ I.D Card
- ☐ Credible Witness
- ☐ Drivers License
- ☐ Known Personally
- ☐ Passport
- ☐ Other:

I.D. Number:

Issued By:

Issued Date:

Expiration Date:

Document Type:

Date/Time Notarized: **AM** **PM**

Document Date:

Fee Charged:

Printed Name and Address of Witness:

Phone Number:

Email:

Witness' Signature:

Comments :

Record Number:

NOTARY RECORD

Printed Name and Address of Signer:	Phone Number:	Thumb Print:
	Email:	
	Signer's Signature:	

Service Performed:	Identification:		I.D. Number:	
☐ Oath	☐ I.D Card	☐ Credible Witness	Issued By:	
☐ Acknowledgment	☐ Drivers License	☐ Known Personally	Issued Date:	Expiration Date:
☐ Jurat	☐ Passport			
☐ Other:	☐ Other:			
Document Type:	Date/Time Notarized: AM PM		Document Date:	Fee Charged:

Printed Name and Address of Witness:	Phone Number:
	Email:
	Witness' Signature:

Comments :	Record Number:

NOTARY RECORD

Printed Name and Address of Signer:	Phone Number:	Thumb Print:
	Email:	
	Signer's Signature:	

Service Performed:	Identification:		I.D. Number:	
☐ Oath	☐ I.D Card	☐ Credible Witness	Issued By:	
☐ Acknowledgment	☐ Drivers License	☐ Known Personally	Issued Date:	Expiration Date:
☐ Jurat	☐ Passport			
☐ Other:	☐ Other:			
Document Type:	Date/Time Notarized: AM PM		Document Date:	Fee Charged:

Printed Name and Address of Witness:	Phone Number:
	Email:
	Witness' Signature:

Comments :	Record Number:

NOTARY RECORD

Printed Name and Address of Signer:	**Phone Number:**	**Thumb Print:**
	Email:	
	Signer's Signature:	

Service Performed: ☐ Oath ☐ Acknowledgment ☐ Jurat ☐ Other:	**Identification:** ☐ I.D Card ☐ Credible Witness ☐ Drivers License ☐ Known Personally ☐ Passport ☐ Other:	**I.D. Number:**	
		Issued By:	
		Issued Date:	**Expiration Date:**
Document Type:	**Date/Time Notarized:** AM PM	**Document Date:**	**Fee Charged:**

Printed Name and Address of Witness:	**Phone Number:**
	Email:
	Witness' Signature:
Comments :	**Record Number:**

NOTARY RECORD

Printed Name and Address of Signer:	**Phone Number:**	**Thumb Print:**
	Email:	
	Signer's Signature:	

Service Performed: ☐ Oath ☐ Acknowledgment ☐ Jurat ☐ Other:	**Identification:** ☐ I.D Card ☐ Credible Witness ☐ Drivers License ☐ Known Personally ☐ Passport ☐ Other:	**I.D. Number:**	
		Issued By:	
		Issued Date:	**Expiration Date:**
Document Type:	**Date/Time Notarized:** AM PM	**Document Date:**	**Fee Charged:**

Printed Name and Address of Witness:	**Phone Number:**
	Email:
	Witness' Signature:
Comments :	**Record Number:**

Made in the USA
Monee, IL
12 November 2026

76ec9630-4e63-4d4a-b30b-07955fe004f7R01